ILLINOIS
Off the Beaten Path

ILLINOIS
Off the Beaten Path

Rod Fensom

Julie Foreman

The
Globe
Pequot
Press

Chester, Connecticut 06412

Library of Congress Cataloging-in-Publication Data

Fensom, Rod.
    Illinois : off the beaten path.

    Includes index.
    1. Illinois — Description and travel — 1981 — Guide —
books. I. Foreman, Julie, 1954-   . II. Title.
F539.3.F46   1987   917.73'0443   86-45969
ISBN 0-88742-026-5 (pbk.)

Manufactured in the United States of America
First Edition/First Printing

Illustrations by Steve Baldwin
Cover illustration:
The Belvedere Mansion, Galena, Illinois.

Typography and Cartography by Raven Type, Inc.

Acknowledgments

The authors would like to thank the Illinois Office of Tourism, chambers of commerce throughout Illinois and a helpful group of correspondents from around the state who contributed a remarkable amount of information on places, sights and attractions here in the Land of Lincoln.

STATE OF ILLINOIS
OFFICE OF THE GOVERNOR
SPRINGFIELD 62706

JAMES R. THOMPSON
GOVERNOR

Greetings:

I wish to personally invite you to visit Illinois. I think you will be delighted to find what fun and enjoyment lies ahead for you and your family in Illinois.

Whether you're seven or seventy, Illinois is the place for a great vacation. Each region of the state offers its own unique qualities and a variety of activities including spectacular scenery, winter sports and festivals, the exciting nightlife of our great Windy City and much, much more.

Once you see what Illinois has to offer, contact an Illinois Tourist Information Center. Our friendly and professional travel counselors will provide you with free literature and answer any questions you might have in planning your Illinois getaway. I invite you to come experience all the fun-filled activities and historic beauty that Illinois has waiting for you to discover.

Sincerely,

James R. Thompson
GOVERNOR

JRT:jj

Illinois

Contents

Introduction

Trips come in all kinds of boxes. There's the big one you open only once in a lifetime . . . a trip to China, for example. Some are neatly done up, thoughtfully planned, all tied together with a tidy bow—the standard-issue European motorcoach tour. But, as they say, good things come in small packages, too.

That's what we're about here, small packages, weekend trips and family vacations right here in our own backyard. What we've sought out, as the title says, are places off the beaten path. We like to think of them as surprises—perfect little jewel boxes that you turn over and over and examine closely—fascinating places filled with unexpected delights you probably wouldn't otherwise come across. Like us, if you're curious, a turner-down-of-back-roads, more than a little inquisitive, given to snooping into things, then you'll enjoy our county-by-county exploration of Illinois. If you don't need a Disneyland or a Las Vegas, you'll come along happily on our statewide travels. We've included a little bit of everything—the state's biggest tree, a two-story outhouse, fishing lakes and campgrounds, historic bits and corners, a golden pyramid and dancing horses. We've written about heavenly country cafes where biscuits and gravy scuttle even the most serious of diets. We've found country inns and guesthouses and even a few farms that welcome city vacationers. What we haven't included are Chicago and Springfield (places decidedly *on* the path), for a number of good guides to those cities exist.

For the not-so-easily persuaded, there's a lot more to Illinois than cornfields and Lincoln. But we're proud of both. Geographically, the state is crisscrossed by waterways, once thoroughfares of commerce, now recreation spots. Along the western border and in the south, the state turns hilly. While we may be the Prairie State, we have mountains and woodlands, as well. The Shawnee National Forest forms a green belt across the state's lower extremity, over the low mountains of the Illinois Ozarks.

When you use this as a guidebook, be sure to plan ahead. Check those attractions you want to visit, because hours and prices change frequently. When you're traveling through the state, ask. We've found the people to be universally friendly and helpful. What's more, we've discovered it's a pretty nice state, one rich in history and architecture, with a wealth of things to see and do—many free. So why not pack up the family and head out on a vacation in your own backyard. For a week or a weekend, there's something unexpected in Illinois.

Off the Beaten Path
in Northeastern Illinois

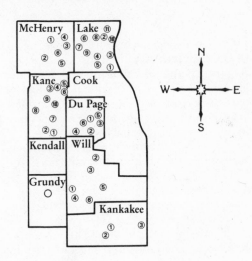

NORTHEAST

Du Page
1. Glen Ellyn
2. Lisle
3. Lombard
4. Naperville
5. Oak Brook
6. Wheaton

Grundy
O Morris

Kane
1. Aurora
2. Batavia
3. Carpentersville
4. Dundee
5. East Dundee
6. Elgin
7. Geneva
8. La Fox
9. South Elgin
10. St. Charles

Kankakee
1. Bourbonnais
2. Kankakee
3. Momence

Lake
1. Deerfield
2. Gurnee
3. Highland Park
4. Libertyville
5. Long Grove
6. Spring Grove
7. Volo
8. Wadsworth
9. Wauconda
10. Waukegan
11. Zion

McHenry
1. Hebron
2. Marengo
3. McHenry
4. Richmond
5. Union
6. Woodstock

Will
1. Braidwood
2. Frankfort
3. Joliet
4. Lockport
5. New Lenox
6. Wilmington

Du Page County

Of what are euphemistically known as the collar counties—those surrounding Cook—Du Page County is surely the white collar enclosing the beefy neck of Chicago, buttoned-down, starched, of oxford cloth. It's conservative, Republican, a place of manicured lawns and solid brick homes (a drive through one of the county's prettiest towns, Elmhurst, will convince you of that).

On its northeast corner, Du Page County slices through **O'Hare International Airport,** on the south it encloses the **Argonne National Laboratory,** and on the west, it bisects the grounds of the **Fermi National Accelerator Laboratory,** the world's largest particle accelerator, where scientists from around the world come to study quirks and quarks. There's a lot going on in the county.

The **Morton Arboretum** offers year-round escape to nature for harried city dwellers. One mile north of Lisle, at the SR 53 exit of the East-West Tollway (SR 5), the garden encompasses 1,500 acres of plants and trees and shrubs. Thirteen miles of footpaths and interpretive trails provide a look at nature. Hours are 9 a.m.–7 p.m. during Daylight Saving Time, 9 a.m.–5 p.m. during the rest of the year. The arboretum has a delightful restaurant, **The Gingko,** open for lunch and tea daily (lunch ranges from $5–$7), and a gift shop; (312) 968-0074.

For history buffs, visiting the **Old Naper Settlement** at 201 W. Porter in Naperville, makes an ideal afternoon. Here, 20 historic buildings on a 12-acre site recreate a nineteenth-century village. Costumed guides lead visitors through an assortment of structures: a windmill, barn, post office, smokehouse and the tiny Gothic Century Memorial Chapel. The **Caroline Martin-Mitchell Mansion,** built in 1883, is listed in the *National Register of Historic Places.* Open May through October, Saturday, Sunday and Wednesday from 1:30– 4:30 p.m.; (312) 420-6010.

Furthermore, the **Old Graue Mill** at York and Spring roads in Oak Brook, is grist for a nostalgic afternoon. It's the only operating waterwheel in the state, and a white-aproned miller turns out stone-ground cornmeal for sale in the country store. Upstairs is a Victorian drawing room, kitchen and children's room with antique dolls and toys. Open 10 a.m.–5 p.m. daily, May through October; (312) 655-2090. Admission, $1, adults; 50 cents, children and seniors.

Wheaton, the county seat, is home to **Wheaton College,** founded in 1853, and the headquarters of a number of religious publishing houses and organizations. Wheaton College is Billy Graham's alma mater and the site of the **Billy Graham Center Museum** with its Walk Through the Gospel and scenes from American evangelism since 1702. Open daily, 9:30 a.m.–5:30 p.m., Friday 1–9 p.m., Sunday 1–5 p.m., closed holidays; (312) 260-5909.

Not every county has its own mastodon, but, at Armerding Hall on campus, a skeleton of the giant Perry Mastodon, which was found locally, is on exhibit; (312) 260-5000.

One of Wheaton's most famous sons is football hero Red Grange. At the **Red Grange Museum/Heritage Gallery,** 421 County Farm Rd., displays and films tell the story of his life; (312) 682-7363. Open Monday through Friday 8 a.m.– 4:30 p.m.

Also in Wheaton is **Cantigny,** the former estate of the late Col. Robert R. McCormick, celebrated publisher of the *Chicago Tribune.* Today, the 500-acre grounds and Georgian mansion are open to the public from 9 a.m. until dusk daily. Picnicking and walks through the formal gardens are popular pastimes. On Sundays, concerts are presented in the library. The **First Infantry Division Museum** here commemorates the division in which the colonel served in World War I. At 15151 Winfield Rd.; (312) 668-5161. Admission is free, guided tours are available. Open 10 a.m.–5 p.m. daily except Monday.

Another free and worthwhile Wheaton attraction is the **Du Page County Historical Museum,** located in an 1891 Romanesque-style limestone structure. Visit the pioneer log cabin, Victorian period rooms, the farm room and the collection of Civil War memorabilia. At 102 E. Wesley St.; (312) 682-7343. Its hours are 10 a.m.–4 p.m. on Monday, Wednesday, Friday and Saturday. Du Page County, in fact, has no shortage of museums—over a dozen in all.

Equally numerous are golf courses, if history's not your game. Du Page boasts 24 public courses, plus a handful of private courses, making it one of the most golf-accessible counties in the state. Each year, the Western Open is played at Oak Brook's **Butler National Golf Club.** This mania is no recent phenomenon. The **Chicago Golf Club,** a private club in Wheaton, claims to have been the first 18-hole course in the United States when it opened in 1892.

Plenty of other outdoor activities are available in Du Page

County, as well. For example, if your interests are somewhat patrician, there are polo matches each Saturday and Sunday afternoon during the summer and fall at the **Oak Brook Polo Club,** York Road at Twenty-second Street in Oak Brook; (312) 571-7656.

During mid-May, Lombard is abloom for the annual **Lilac Festival,** making it one of the best smelling towns in the county. Parades are scheduled and a Lilac Queen is named. Call (312) 629-3799 for more information.

Especially pleasant is the **Illinois Prairie Path,** beginning in Elmhurst at York Road south of North Avenue. This 45-mile-long biking and hiking trail follows an old railroad right-of-way, where wildflowers, prairie grasses, tiny parks and rest stops are plentiful; (312) 665-5310.

At Glen Ellyn, the **Willowbrook Wildlife Haven,** 525 S. Park Blvd., is always popular with children. Here, wounded, lost and captured native wildlife are cared for. Guided tours and educational talks are given. Its hours are from 9 a.m.–5 p.m. daily; (312) 790-4900. Admission is free.

The county's forest preserves are among the finest in the area, with 30 preserves encompassing 17,500 acres. At various locations you'll find dog training fields, model airplane runs, bird-watching facilities, cross-country skiing, ice skating, hiking and equestrian fields.

· **Oak Brook Center,** Twenty-second Street and SR 83, is one of the Chicago area's outstanding regional centers with Marshall Field's, Sak's Fifth Avenue, and Neiman-Marcus as major tenants. More than 100 shops and restaurants are laid out around a landscaped courtyard.

Grundy County

Perhaps nothing demonstrates quite as eloquently the changes in our society as the juxtaposition of the historic and the futuristic. In Morris, the seat of Grundy County, the towering shapes of the Dresden Nuclear Power Station form a striking contrast to the waters of the old Illinois and Michigan (I&M) Canal, which flow past town and through **Gebhard Woods State Park.**

The 30-acre park, named after its donor, Fred Gebhard, is situated off SR 47 at the southwest edge of Morris on the north bank of the I&M Canal (see Will County). The park has four ponds for children's fishing plus adult fishing in the canal and in Nettle Creek, which forms the north and east boundaries of the park. Largemouth bass, bluegill, sunfish and catfish are caught. With an impressive collection of shade trees—walnut, oak, cottonwood, ash and maple—picnicking is a popular activity here. Gebhard Woods is part of the I&M Canal State Trail and the I&M Canal National Heritage Corridor. For further information, contact the Site Superintendent, Gebhard Woods State Park, P.O. Box 272, Morris, IL 60450; (815) 942-0796.

Just one mile west of Gebhard Woods is the largest tree in Illinois, on the south side of the canal. The monumental eastern cottonwood measures 120 feet high, with a circumference of 27 feet 4 inches.

East of Morris, in Evergreen Cemetery, lies the grave of **Shabbona** (1775–1859), the chief of the Potawatomi tribe, who sided with the settlers during the Black Hawk War of 1832. Even though a proven friend, Shabbona and his tribe were forced to move to a reservation in Kansas in 1836. He later returned to Illinois. The city of Morris honors the Indian hero with one of the last working steam pump fire engines in the country, **Old Shab-a-nee,** in use from 1868 to 1922 and appearing today in parades.

The last weekend in September Morris hosts the **Grundy County Corn Festival,** one of the largest county agricultural festivals in the state. Parades, exhibits, musical concerts and paddlewheel boat excursions on the Illinois River take second billing to the star of the show—truckloads of fresh sweet corn. Call (815) 942-CORN for information.

About eight miles southeast of Morris and south of the Illinois River, is **Goose Lake Prairie State Park,** one of the last remnants of prairie left in this, the prairie state, and one of the largest preserves in the tall grass region of North America. As such, it has national significance. Of its 2,357 acres, 1,513 are dedicated as an Illinois Nature Preserve.

There is, however, no lake at Goose Lake, having been drained at the end of the last century for farming and for the clay deposits under it. Instead, the grasses and flowers are much like what the state's earliest settlers would have encountered. The palette of wildflowers changes in hue throughout the seasons: in spring, the violet shooting star and blue-eyed grass; in summer, false indigo and blazing star; and in fall, asters and goldenrods.

The park's Tallgrass Nature Trail offers a fascinating walk through 1½ miles of prairie, across potholes and marshes and a unique floating bridge.

A two-story replica of the 1834–35 John Cragg cabin, nick-named the **Palace,** stands in the park. The original was a station on the underground railroad.

An interpretive program is offered year-round. The park's address, on Jugtown Road, comes from an early settlement here. Dating from 1853, Jugtown was a small community whose inhabitants made drain tiles, water jugs, and pottery from the region's clay. For information on the park, contact the Site Superintendent, 5010 N. Jugtown Rd., Morris, IL 60450; (815) 942-2899.

Kane County

One man could be credited almost solely with the settlement of the Fox River Valley, although that was certainly not his intention. Chief Black Hawk of the Sauk Indians was among the least friendly of the Indian leaders in the area that is now Illinois. In the War of 1812, he sided with the British against the Americans. The encroachment of white settlers on his traditional lands led to the tragic Black Hawk War of 1832 in which the Sauk and Fox tribes were virtually exterminated.

Soldiers returning east from this frontier battle spoke highly of the fertile land along the river. Thus communities sprung up beside the waterway, notably Geneva in 1833, as supply centers for area farms and pioneers traveling further west.

For the weekend traveler on nothing more than a sightseeing excursion, a trip through the Kane County towns of the Fox River is richly rewarding. Follow SR 31 along the eastern edge of the county as it meanders along next to the Fox River. In the south, begin with Aurora.

Here, the best show in town is the **Paramount Arts Centre,** 23 E. Galena Blvd. On an island in the Fox River, the stylish old art deco movie palace was built in 1931 by noted theater architects Rapp and Rapp as a romanticized version of Venice. A 70-foot cascade light marquee adorns the red brick and terra-cotta exterior. The Paramount was restored in 1978 and protected in the *National Register of Historic Places* two years later. Movies and live entertainment fill the bill today. Call

(312) 896-6666 for program information.

West of town on Galena Boulevard (and about 2½ miles west of Randall Road) is the Fox Valley Park District's **Blackberry Historical Farm-Village**. From what was once a dairy farm has been fashioned a unique park with a collection of rides and historic exhibits. It receives high marks as an ideal spot for family outings.

Pony rides and an antique carousel vie for junior horsemen. A miniature steam train, Old Engine #9, takes visitors around the 60-acre park and Lake Gregory to an 1840 Pioneer Farm. A petting barn with barnyard animals, hay wagon rides and a Pioneer Log Cabin where craftsmen demonstrate frontier skills are part of the attraction.

Museums on the property exhibit early carriages, a one-room schoolhouse and Victorian women's furnishings. Throughout the season, special events such as a **Bluegrass Festival**, a **Blacksmithing Weekend** and an **Indian Summer Day** are scheduled. Open daily 10 a.m.– 4:30 p.m. May to Labor Day, weekends to mid-October. Admission, adults $3.50; children, $3; (312) 892-1550.

Back in Aurora, one of the most unusual museums in the Fox Valley is the **Grand Army of the Republic Hall and Museum,** 23 E. Downer. The castellated limestone building with a statue of a Civil War soldier on top was built in 1877 and is listed in the *National Register of Historic Places*. Cannons line the front yard of the museum, which looks something like a church. Inside, Civil War memorabilia is the focus of the collection. Open 1–4 p.m. Monday, Wednesday and Friday; (312) 897-7221.

North of Aurora in Batavia is **Fermilab**, the world's largest particle accelerator. A free self-guided tour is offered seven days a week from 8:30 a.m.–5 p.m. Included is a fascinating 13-minute movie that explains the workings of the research center. The tour begins on the 15th floor of the Robert Rathbun Wilson Hall, with a view out over the entire complex. Complete the tour in your car, driving through the Fermilab facility (no public access to buildings in this area). Keep an eye out for the center's buffalo herd, some 85 strong, a historical counterpoint to the high-tech activities of the laboratory; (312) 840-3000.

Just down the road, at 14 N. Washington Ave. in Batavia, is the 1885 Alexander Grimes farmhouse. The lovely old Victorian is home to **The Savery Shops,** a collection of 12 dealers and artists. Open daily from 10 a.m.–5 p.m. and Sunday from noon–5 p.m.; (312) 879-6825.

Continuing north on SR 31, Geneva is the next stop. Its historic district is a bonanza of period architecture with more than 200 structures listed in the *National Register of Historic Places*. Geneva is the county seat, and the 1891 **Kane County Courthouse** is historically significant, with unique wrought iron balconies gracing the first to the fourth interior floors. Founded as a trading center, Geneva is still that, with dozens of charming shops.

Shakespeare and the classics come to the Fox River each summer, as the **Renaissance Repertory Company** in Geneva presents outdoor theater at Island Park; (312) 232-0371.

One of the oldest annual festivals in the state, Geneva's **Swedish Days** is held each June to commemorate the area's Swedish heritage. Quilts, crafts, *rösemaling* (Swedish painted flower decoration) and an unforgettable Swedish buffet are part of the fun.

While it might not be fair to the other towns along the way, we think St. Charles is the jewel of the Fox River. Here, pretty wooded slopes fall away to the slow-running river where the Fox River Trail (a bicycle and walking path ten miles long from St. Charles to Aurora) hugs the water. It's the perfect walking town, bisected by a river, with plenty of shops and side streets to explore. It's nice to see a small town where things are going well, business is thriving, the economy healthy. You come away with an almost Disney-like impression of a town where clean streets and smiling faces are part of the package.

St. Charles's claim to fame is antiquing. **Giant Antique Markets I, II** and **III** are dealer cooperatives with a remarkable collection of stuff under each roof.

On the first Sunday of each month, the **Kane County Flea Market** takes over the County Fairgrounds with 1,400 dealers on 25 acres, attracting 15,000 or so shoppers. It has been called the largest flea market in the world, perhaps rightly so. The market ignores the weather and never cancels. Its success is the work of Helen Robinson, a 68-year-old grandmother who actively supervises the monthly operation, including three kitchens and eight food trailers to feed the bargain hunters. Located on Randall Road just south of SR 64; (312) 377-2252. Open 7 a.m.–4 p.m. Admission, $2 for shoppers.

Shoppers, too, will enjoy the three restored areas in town—

Old St. Charles, Century Corners and **Fox Island Square,** designed around the original Howell factory brick chimney. Lunch is a welcome respite, and the choices of restaurants are numerous. For something simple, try the **Inglenook Pantry,** a real Pennsylvania Dutch family buffet where chef-owner John Weaver holds forth. Inexpensive. Open Sunday through Friday 11 a.m.–2 p.m., Saturday 11:30 a.m.–3 p.m., and Friday and Saturday evenings from 5:30–8:30 p.m. for dinner; (312) 377-0373.

Or, try as we did, the cozy **Old Church Inn,** 18 N. Fourth St., which is just what it sounds like. Formerly St. Patrick's Catholic Church, the limestone structure was erected in 1851. Seating is in the original church pews. Owners Toni and Sam Alex have transformed the interior with stained glass and antiques into an airy country dining room. Try the Friday night fish fry with memorable clam chowder for $5.95. Or, perhaps Shrimp Polanaise—sauteed with shallots, mushrooms, Chablis, sour cream and heavy cream. Apart from the fish fry, dinners range from $6.50–$13.

The handsome old 1928 **Baker Hotel,** a *National Register* building, serves only a Sunday brunch in its one-of-a-kind ballroom for $5.95, from 10 a.m.–1:30 p.m. A string quartet entertains. The oval room has a back-lit colored glass floor and a view of the river. The Moorish stucco interiors lead out onto a terrace with a gazebo that's perfect for photographing the waterfalls behind the hotel. At 100 W. Main St.; (312) 584-2100.

But to *really* get the feel of the river, you have to get out on it. And the best way to do that is a ride on *St. Charles Belle,* a 132-passenger paddlewheeler. Adults, $2; children, $1. Mid-May through mid-October, the excursion boat leaves from Pottawatomie Park at 3:30 p.m. on weekdays and at 2, 3, and 4 p.m. on Sundays. Call (312) 584-2334. Also in this hilly, tidy park north of downtown is a swimming pool, a miniature golf course, tennis courts and a miniature train ride for youngsters (75 cents).

Professional entertainment in St. Charles is offered at the **Dellora A. Norris Cultural Arts Center,** 1040 Dunham Rd., (312) 584-7200, and at **Pheasant Run,** a resort complex east of town on SR 64; (312) 584-1454. Both feature name entertainers and shows.

Just west of St. Charles in La Fox is the **Garfield Farm and Tavern Museum,** a living farm of the 1840s. Roosters wander in and out of the weathered barns. Herbs and flowers grow in the curator's garden. In 1841, Timothy and Harriet Frost Garfield brought their eight children from Vermont to the prairie lands of Illinois. In 1977, the third generation owner, Elva Ruth Garfield, donated the farm as a museum, one of the most intact historical sites in the country, one used for ongoing archeological studies. It's the largest Illinois farm in the *National Register of Historic Places* and it gives the visitor an excellent idea of just how a farm family of the 1840s must have lived. Walk through the grounds and the interior of the brick (made locally) home and tavern with curator Jerome Johnson and his wife Holly. The first weekend in October is the three-day **Fall Festival** with historic music, a storyteller, blacksmithing, craft demonstrations and hearty farm cooking appropriate to the period. Open 1–4 p.m. on Wednesday and Sunday, year-round or by appointment. Adults, $2; children, $1. Call (312) 584-8485.

Further north on SR 31, in South Elgin, is the **Fox River Trolley Museum**, where you can take a three-mile, 30-minute ride along the Fox River on this electric railway. Vintage railway cars are on display. Open Sunday, 11 a.m.–6 p.m. May through October, Saturday in July and August 1–5 p.m.; (312) 697-4676. The museum is on SR 31 in South Elgin, three blocks south of State Street.

In Elgin, don't go looking for the Elgin Watch Factory, since 1866 the manufacturer of America's best known timepieces. It closed in 1965. What you can explore, however, is the **Elgin Historic District.** The *National Register* district includes 667 structures, many of noteworthy architecture—Greek Revival, Queen Anne, Shingle style, and brick row houses. A walking tour map is available from the Elgin Visitors Bureau; (312) 741-5660.

Another important industry for Elgin was the dairy business, and it was here that Gail Borden invented his process for condensing milk in 1856.

The Dundee area, just north of Elgin, claims its famous sons as well. Allan Pinkerton, famous detective and head of the Union Army's spy service in the Civil War, lived here from 1844–50. A historical marker indicates the site on Third Street in West Dundee. Evangelist Billy Sunday owned the farm on which his wife was born in Sleepy Hollow, just west on SR 72.

In Dundee, tour the **Haeger Potteries Factory** at 7 Maiden Lane. From the banks of the Fox River, the company founder took clay to use in his Dundee Brickyards in 1871 to make bricks that were used to rebuild Chicago after the Great Chicago Fire. Tours available Monday through Thursday, 45 minutes, free; (312) 426-3441. Factory outlet open Monday through Friday, 8 a.m.–5 p.m.; Saturday and Sunday, 10 a.m.–5 p.m.

Santa's Village, SR 25 and SR 72 in East Dundee, is a popular amusement park for children with petting zoo, more than 30 rides and shows. Open daily mid-June to Labor Day, weekends mid-May through September. Hours are 10 a.m.–6 p.m. weekdays, 11 a.m.–7 p.m. weekends. Admission, $7.95; (312) 426-6751.

One of Fox Valley's most popular restaurants, **The Milk Pail,** is also located in East Dundee. The 40-year-old family favorite features country cooking with specialities such as breast of pheasant, trout, duck and fresh baked goods. At SR 25, closed Monday, (312) 742-5040, dinners range from $6.95–$12.50.

Carpentersville, in the northeast corner of Kane County, is the last stop. Here, rent a raft or canoe at **Fox Floats,** located at Lincoln Avenue and the Carpentersville Dam. The two-hour trips are some of the best ways to see the river scenery. The sunset candlelight raft trip is especially pleasant. Prices from $17–$20; (312) 428-6811.

Kankakee County

The Kankakee River, the namesake of the county and city, offers more than just scenic beauty. Six miles northwest of Kankakee on SR 102, along the river's banks is the **Kankakee River State Park,** 2,780 wooded acres spread out along 11 miles of the river. The first European to travel down that river was Rene Robert Cavalier, Sieur de la Salle, who, with a party of 14 men, traveled from the headwaters of the Kankakee down to the Illinois River in 1679.

Modern explorers make the trip downstream daily throughout the summer on one of the cleanest waterways in the state. **Reed's Canoe Trips,** 907 N. Indiana Ave., Kankakee, books canoe trips from three hours to three days. Canoes, paddles, life jackets and return transportation are provided. The service operates daily from April 1 to October 15; (815) 932-2663.

The state park's Rock Creek Canyon is especially pretty with its picturesque waterfall and gnarled cedars growing from its steep limestone walls. Hiking, equestrian and snowmobile trails

Bradley House, Kankakee

are laced throughout the park's forested acres. Picnic facilities and camping (with electric hookup) are available. Hunting and fishing are seasonal sports in the park. In the summer, the park rangers present an informative interpretive program. For information, contact the Park Ranger, R.R. 1, Bourbonnais, IL 60914; (815) 933-1383.

Each July, fishermen from around the Midwest gather to try their luck at angling in the annual **Kankakee River Valley Fishing Derby.** More than $40,000 is awarded in prizes to those who land the tagged fish. For more information, call 1-800-892-6450 in Illinois, (815) 935-7390 outside the state.

Golf, too, has its proponents and Kankakee County has the courses to satisfy even the most avid. There are seven courses, including the **Bon Vivant Country Club** (815) 935-0403, ranked second in the district only after Butler National by the Chicago District Golf Association.

During Labor Day weekend, the **Kankakee River Valley Regatta** brings powerboats to the river from miles around for fast and wonderful racing championships.

In the southwest part of Kankakee, at Eighth Avenue and Water Street, is the boyhood home of Len Small, 28th governor of Illinois. Situated on a 22-acre park, the home is part of the **Kankakee Historical Society Museum.** The 1855 Italianate limestone building has been restored and rooms furnished in period style. On the grounds, visitors can tour a historic one-room schoolhouse. Admission is free. Open year-round 10 a.m.–3 p.m. Monday through Friday and 1–4 p.m. on Saturday and Sunday.

Another cultural pursuit in town is the **Kankakee Valley Theater,** a local community theater, which schedules performances throughout the year. Call (815) 935-8510.

Kankakee's **Bradley House,** at Harrison and the river, was designed by Frank Lloyd Wright as a private residence, the first in his famous "Prairie style." The 1901 structure is true to form with long, low lines and overhanging gables. Set in a grove of trees on the Kankakee River, the effect is a natural, harmonious one. Wright designed the original furnishings, china and rugs for the home, too. In 1953, the architectural showplace became a charming inn, run by two army cooks. It's no longer open as a restaurant, but plans are underway to reopen the landmark. Call the visitor's bureau for details: (800) 892-6450 in Illinois; (815) 935-7390, out of state.

Dining in a historic setting is available, however, at the **Bennett-Curtis House,** 302 W. Taylor St. in Grant Park, northeast of Kankakee. The 1900 Victorian is the former home of Illinois Sen. Edward C. Curtis. Antiques are everywhere around you as you dine on a menu of gourmet selections by reservation only. Open for lunch Tuesday through Saturday, noon seating; dinner on Friday and Saturday, seating at 7:30 p.m. Call (815) 465-6025 for reservations. Dinner has a fixed price, $30. Sunday brunch is served from 11 a.m.–2 p.m. You may bring your own wine.

Bourbonnais, just north of Kankakee, was one of the earliest settlements on the Kankakee River, dating from the founding of a French trading post here in 1832. An influx of French Canadians followed, giving the region its French flavor. In Bourbonnais is the **Olivet Nazarene College** (formerly the Catholic St. Viator College), with its renowned **Strickler Planetarium;** (815) 939-5395. More than 4,800 stars are projected onto a 30-foot dome in a series of seasonal programs. Most programs are written and produced by astronomy students at the college. Admission, adults, $1; children, 75 cents.

Momence, too, is a historic community, once known as the Old Border Town (between wilderness and civilization), situated on the Hubbard Trail linking Fort Dearborn (Chicago) to Vincennes, Indiana. The road, also known as the Vincennes Trail, was designated a state road, later Illinois 1.

Momence today boasts a number of historic homes. The **Momence Historic House,** 117 N. Dixie Highway, is a furnished home that lets the visitor see what life was like in the period 1870–1900. The kitchen, with its dry sink and pump, pie safe and butter churn, speaks of a time without modern appliances. Open April through early December, Saturday and Sunday only. Free; (815) 472-6951.

A major industry in Momence is the growing of gladiolus—more than 150,000 are harvested annually. In early August, the **Momence Gladiolus Festival** draws thousands from across the country. In addition to lovely flowers, there are parades, antique car shows and the oldest continuous drum and bugle corps competition in the United States. Call (815) 472-4620 for more information.

Lake County

The character of Lake County changes at about the halfway point—from a collection of commuter bedroom communities to rural Illinois. At its lower edge are a number of the Chicago area's most affluent suburbs, such as Highland Park, Lake Forest, Deerfield and Barrington. The county even claims the second greatest buying power in the United States at $34,428 per household average. At its northern border lies Wisconsin and to the east, Lake Michigan. Other lakes, too, are never far away—more than 120 fishing and boating lakes in the county, including **Chain O'Lakes State Park.** Open year-round, the park has 220 campsites, some with electric hookup, showers, boat rental, fishing and a playground. Go hunting from November to mid-December and horseback riding from May 1 to October. Snowmobiling and cross-country skiing are popular during the winter months. At 39947 N. State Park Road, Spring Grove, IL 60081; (312) 587-5512.

Illinois Beach State Park is only 20 miles east of Chain

The Gold Pyramid House, Wadsworth

O'Lakes, on Lake Michigan at Zion. The park's primary feature is a seven-mile stretch of beach with Illinois's last and best natural lakeshore dunes area. The **Illinois Beach Resort and Conference Center** is located on the grounds of the state park. With health club, gourmet dining room and an indoor swimming pool, it has some of the fanciest accommodations in any state park. The park is on Sheridan and Wadsworth roads. The center's phone number is (312) 249-2100; the park's number is (312) 662-4811.

Appropriate to its name, Zion hosts the **Zion Passion Play** each year at the Christian Arts Auditorium. Performances are scheduled every Saturday in April and May and on Good Friday. Tickets are $7 for adults and $5 for students and senior citizens; (312) 746-2221.

In Libertyville is a very special place called **The Lambs** (SR 176, east of I-94). It is a nonprofit organization dedicated to helping mentally handicapped adults. The Lambs is both a residence and a workplace where vocational training and employment are provided. More than 106 residents work in The Lambs's eight businesses at the 51-acre farm. Each year, a quarter of a million people visit Lambs Farm for special events and to sample the products made by the residents. Shop at the pet shop housed in a turn-of-the-century barn, the thrift shop or country store, the silk screen shop or Grandma's Bakery. One of the most popular of The Lambs's offerings is **The Country Inn,** a wonderful old-fashioned restaurant with hearty home cooking. Open daily for lunch at 11 a.m. Dinner is served Tuesday through Saturday until 8:30 p.m. On Sunday, brunch is served 11 a.m.–2:30 p.m., dinner 4–7 p.m. (Dinners range from $4–$12.) For reservations, call (312) 362-5050.

Also in Libertyville is the **Dave Adler Cultural Center** at 1700 N. Milwaukee; (312) 367-0707. Adler, an architect, built this 23-room house about 1920, and it is now home to art exhibits and occasional concerts. The dining room has been restored with original furnishings. Open year-round 1–4 p.m. Admission free.

What was formerly the farm of Illinois's most political family, the Adlai Stevensons, is here in Libertyville as well, now part of the Lake County Forest Preserve.

Bigger even than the herd at Vienna's famous Spanish Riding School, **Tempel Farms's** stable of the handsome Lipizzan stallions is the world's largest, right here in Wadsworth, Illinois. Catch a rare demonstration of equine talent at the 6,000-acre Tempel Farms. Performances are held Sundays at 1 p.m. and Wednesdays at 10:30 a.m. from the end of May through July and from the end of August until the first of October. Performances lasting an hour and 15 minutes are held regardless of the weather. No reserved seating, adults, $7; children 4–12, $4; under 3, free. At 15280 Wadsworth Road; (312) 623-7272.

Cleopatra's ghost! Also in Wadsworth is the unique **Gold Pyramid House.** Built by contractor James Onan, the 55-foot, 24K gold-plated pyramid is probably one of the most unusual residences in Illinois, if not the country. With a 200-ton statue of *Ramses II* standing guard, the structure is protected, too, by a spring-fed moat. It's oriented to true north, as is its model, the Great Pyramid of Cheops in Egypt. Inside is a collection of Egyptian-styled furniture and art. Open weekends only July 4th through Labor Day, 11 a.m.–5 p.m. Adults, $6, children 12 and under, $3; (312) 662-6666. Take I-94 north to SR 132, exit eastbound to Dilley's Road, turn left.

Another family entertainment—one with plenty of "show biz"—is **Six Flags Great America** in Gurnee, the single most popular amusement theme park in Illinois. Bugs Bunny, musical stage reviews and the world's biggest and fastest double racing wooden roller coaster bring families by the thousands each summer. Theme villages, 150 rides and plenty of entertainment and food make it a sure bet for a Lake County outing. Open weekends only from the end of April, then daily mid-May through Labor Day and on weekends only through mid-October. Opens 10 a.m., closes at varying times. Ages 4–54, $14.95; over 55, $9.95; 3 and under, free. At Gurnee, on Grand Avenue (SR 132), one mile east of I-94.

Long Grove (at SR 83 and SR 53 in the southern part of the county), they say, invites you to turn your watch back to yesteryear. The historic village was settled in the 1840s by a group of German farmers who found it much like their own Alsatian homeland. Even after World War I, they continued to speak Plattedeutsch and to tend their farms. The village grew up as a place for farmers to buy their supplies, weigh their milk, make their cheese at the cooperative, and have their horses shod. In 1847, they built a tiny church on a hill near town, where services are still held today.

Antiques seem to be everywhere you look in Long Grove now, with one of the best collections of shops anywhere. The **Long Grove Apple Haus** presses its own cider, makes heavenly apple butter and jam and should be a definite stop; (312) 634-0730. **Long Grove Confectionery**, on the other hand, is famous for hand-dipped chocolates. Try a fat, juicy chocolate-covered strawberry on for size; (312) 634-0080.

More sweet delights are just down the road at the **Sara Lee Bakeries** visitors' center, 500 Waukegan Rd., in Deerfield. See a four-story freezer with 8 million cakes. Call (312) 945-2525 for reservations. A slide program, product demonstration, and refreshments are offered by appointment. Free.

Each summer, the acclaimed Chicago Symphony Orchestra migrates north to Highland Park, taking up residence in their summer home, the **Ravinia Park Musical Festival.** Since 1916, the outdoor music festival has featured a wide variety of classical and popular programs, including renowned guest artists, ballet and chamber music. Take a picnic and lie on the lawn for music under the stars. Call (312) 728-4642 for reservations and prices. Late June through mid-September.

Settled in 1835, Waukegan has a rich history well worth exploring. Originally an Indian village and then a French trading post, its name means "Little Fort" in the local Indian dialect. In 1860, Lincoln, interrupted by fire, delivered what came to be known as his "unfinished speech" here. Today, a bit of that past remains in **Old Waukegan,** a designated Historic District along North Avenue and Franklin streets. For more history, the **Waukegan Historical Society,** 1917 N. Sheridan Rd., is open Wednesdays and Fridays 10 a.m. –2:30 p.m.; (312) 336-1859.

At 414 N. Sheridan Rd., the white-pillared Greek Revival structure is home to the Lake County Chamber of Commerce. Built in 1847 by carriage maker **John Swartout,** the house is in the *National Register of Historic Places.* Today, the Northern Illinois Tourism Council is based here also, and free maps, guides and travel information are available; (312) 249-3800.

If fishing is more to your taste, Waukegan is one of the two main Illinois ports for charter boats. Call (312) BIG-FISH for information on day and overnight trips for chinook and coho salmon. In June, the city sponsors a **Coho Fishing Derby** with daily prizes.

Just south of Waukegan and North Chicago is the **Great Lakes Naval Training Center,** Sheridan Road at SR 137. This 1,500-acre installation is the Navy's largest, even though it's 1,000 miles from salt water! Each Friday is a graduation ceremony for recruits at 1 p.m. Free. Call (312) 688-2201.

At the western edge of the county, in the little town of Volo, U.S. 12 and SR 120, the **Antique Auto Museum** has on display more than 100 classic motor cars and carriages. And if you're souvenir-minded, the showroom has mint condition, but expensive, classic autos for sale; (815) 385-3644. Hours are 10 a.m.–5 p.m. daily, closed Tuesday. Admission is $2.95 adults; children 4–12, $1.50.

One of the area's best pick-your-own fruit farms is **Wauconda Orchards** at 1201 Gossell Rd. in Wauconda, just east of U.S. 12. During the late spring and summer, you might find black raspberries, red raspberries, strawberries or a handful of apple varieties just waiting to be picked; (312) 526-8553. The orchards are open 10 a.m.–5 p.m. daily year-round.

McHenry County

The lucky people of Union—all 600 or so—have more to see and do than many in much larger towns. Fairly close to almost nothing, Union boasts three major museums, each with a busy calendar of special events, and a collection of antique shops to suit every taste.

To start with, the **McHenry County Historical Museum** is right on Main Street (6422 Main St.) in the middle of town. The log cabin in the front yard makes it even more difficult to miss. The 1847 structure was built by Luke Gannon on a site five miles northeast of Huntley, in the southern part of the county, and donated to the museum in 1964 by the family. A program of pioneer exhibitions is held here during the season. The museum also houses a collection of nineteenth-century musical instruments, ladies' fashions and handiwork, farm equipment and Civil War memorabilia. An 1870 school building is part of the museum complex. Open May, September and October on Wednesday and Sunday 1:30– 4:30 p.m.; June, July and August on Wednesday, Saturday and Sunday 1:30– 4:30 p.m. Admission, adults $2, seniors and children, $1. Call for information on specially scheduled events; (815) 923-2267.

Just around the corner and a bit east of town on Olson Road in the middle of cornfields is one of our most-recommended museums in northern Illinois, the **Illinois Railway Museum.** The reasons for its popularity are severalfold: The attraction pleases all senses. You can touch the solid, worn seats as you sit back and enjoy a short train ride. You can enjoy the tingle of excitement as the train bell rings, the whistle blows. And you can watch with loving affection, as most visitors do, as the old steam engine comes puffing into the station. The Railway Museum is a nonprofit organization run by volunteers, train buffs who love the thrill of classic locomotives as much as we do. And most importantly, the exhibit is someplace the whole family can find fun. It's open air, with plenty of places to go—56 acres worth—cars to ride, noises to hear and even a spot for picnics.

When is a train more than a train? Well, when it's one of the museum's 200 cars and locomotives, which include electric interurbans, streetcars, trolleys, diesels, Chicago elevated cars and even a complete silver Burlington Zephyr streamliner. It's one of only two places in the state you can ride a steam engine (the other's in Monticello). One of the most exotic stars of the show is the Russian Decapod from the Frisco Railroad, built in 1917 by Baldwin for the czarist Russian government, but, due to a revolution, never delivered.

Dating from 1851, the depot originally served as the station in Marengo. Behind it are the gift shop and bookstore with a mountain of railroad lore. Throughout the summer are special events, such as the **July 4th Trolley Pageant, Railroad Day,** and **Diesel Day.** From Memorial Day to Labor Day, the museum is open daily 11 a.m.–5 p.m. In May and September, it's open weekends only; in April and October, openings are limited to Sundays. For a ride on the steam train, plan to visit on a summer weekend when the trains run hourly. Admission includes unlimited rides: $4.50 adults, $2.25 children, those under five years of age are admitted free; (815) 923-2488.

South of town, at 8512 S. Union, is **Seven Acres Antique Village and Museum.** It's like someone's attic. Someone who collected almost everything. One of the country's largest antique phonograph collections can be found here along with records, cylinders and needles.

War souvenirs are an important part of the collection, too. Perhaps the best known is the recently added "Hitler photo album." The red-leather-bound treasure has 68 photographs of Hitler and his regiment in World War I. Along with it is a letter written on Hitler's stationery by an American GI to a friend at home and bound copies of *Mein Kampf* found in Hitler's apartment in 1945 after the fall of Berlin.

Military uniforms, including an unusual collection of women's uniforms from the WACS, WAVES and the nurse corps, are featured. And, too, for the military-minded, guns, daggers and helmets aplenty.

A nickelodeon shows movies throughout the day right around the corner from the "Street of Yesteryear," a collection of old-time shops. Outside, the village has its own saloon, blacksmith shop, and pioneer cabin. Desperadoes shoot it out daily during the summer months in a flashy gunfight show. And conveniently nearby is the gallows, a real Chicago version, from the old Cook County jail on Hubbard Street, still waiting for "Terrible Tommy" O'Connor who escaped on Dec. 11, 1921, four days before his scheduled execution, the last one by hanging in the state. To record your day in the past, make a date with the photography studio, where you can get up in Victorian garb, or Wild West attire and have a sepia-toned souvenir in a matter of minutes. Call (815) 923-2214. Open daily April through September 9 a.m.–6 p.m., weekends only in October, 10 a.m.–5 p.m. Closed November through March. Admission, $3.50 adults, $1.75 children. There is an additional charge on those weekends when gunfights are scheduled.

But if *shopping* is your particular passion, stop back in town at the **Village Depot Antiques,** 17603 Depot St. It's run by Mike Donley of the same family that owns **Seven Acres Antique Village.** Taking an old freight depot, later a feed and coal store, and spending two years renovating it, he's fashioned a stylish shop with a good selection of antiques and what are called "collectibles." We especially like the salt and pepper shaker collection. Open daily except Monday 10 a.m.–5 p.m.; (815) 923-2590.

In the center of the county is Woodstock, the county seat, named after the Vermont town from which many of its early citizens came. In the center of the town is the square, not with a courthouse (which is off to one side), but with a handsome park complete with bandstand, spring house and statue dedicated to "the soldiers of 1861–65, in honor of our nation's defenders."

On one side of the brick-paved square is the **Opera House,** an 1890 structure in the *National Register of Historic Places* (121 Van Buren). With its tall tower and ornate interior, its style has been called "Steamboat Gothic." Paul Newman and Orson Welles, who attended school in Woodstock, began their careers here. A seasonal schedule of performances is offered; (815) 338-5300.

On the other side of the square is the old courthouse and jail, now converted into a small shopping gallery upstairs, where **The Seasoned Chef,** a fancy cookware and antique shop, shares space with **Witherspoon's,** a clothing store for country gentry. Downstairs is the **Old Court House Inn,** a fine restaurant with an especially good Sunday brunch (we overindulged in biscuits and gravy). Their booths are the old oak seats from the courthouse where spectators once awaited decisions of the court. Dinners range from $9–$16; (815) 338-6700. The **Jailhouse Saloon** is where a number of Chicago characters, including Eugene Debs, were once held when the place was a real jail. A stone on the side of the courthouse tells us that all this is only 954 feet above sea level.

Driving north from the brick-paved square at Woodstock, take SR 47 to Hebron, where even the perennial optimism of the Chicago Cubs fans is outdone by the Hebron **water tower,** painted to resemble a basketball with the notice that *this* is the home of the 1952 State Champions.

Just east of Hebron on SR 173 is Richmond, only blocks south of the Wisconsin state line. The legendary antique village is chockablock with antique shops of every description. Head first, though, for **Ed's,** 10321 Main St. At a special request, the proprietor will turn on his 1902 Wurlitzer military band organ, once the center of a merry-go-round. The drums and cymbals and glockenspiel add up to the happiest—and loudest—sound in town, commanding the attention of shoppers inside and outside his store; (815) 678-2911. Ed's is open Monday through Saturday 10:30 a.m.–5 p.m. and Sunday from noon–5 p.m. Whatever your weakness, chances are it will find you here— from Victorian wicker, to Spanish doubloons, to china dolls, to Mrs. Anderson's heavenly homemade chocolates.

Since 1919, **Anderson's Homemade Candies,** 10301 Main St., has been bringing them in for hand-dipped English toffees, meltaway fudge and old-fashioned "candy bars" that are really chocolate-covered apricot, orange peel, pudding or krispy rice. Open daily 9 a.m.–5 p.m., Sunday noon–5 p.m. Closed Monday and two weeks in January.

The town holds special exhibits, such as a quilt show and an art glass exhibit, throughout the summer months. Call the Richmond Memorial Hall for more information; (815) 678-4040.

A moraine, according to Webster, is "a mass of rocks, gravel, sand ... carried or deposited by a glacier." And that's exactly what you'll find at **Moraine Hills State Park,** three miles south of McHenry. Lake Defiance, in the park, was created by a chunk of glacier left to melt there. Unusual natural features include a leatherleaf bog—120 acres of floating spagnum moss and leatherleaf surrounded by a moat of open water. The pike marsh contains the largest known colony of pitcher plants in Illinois along with cattails and bullrushes. It's a protected nature preserve and, as such, attracts a rich variety of wildlife as well. Visitors will want to stop at the interpretive center, which explains the park's natural resources. The Pike Marsh Nature Trail features a floating boardwalk perfect for exploration of park plantlife. All state parks are open year-round except Christmas and New Year's days. Contact the Site Superintendent, 914 S. River Rd., McHenry, IL 60050; (815) 385-1624.

Schutten-Aldrich House, Wilmington

Will County

Will County's seat, Joliet, may call to mind only the Blues Brothers and an infamous state prison (part of the movie was set here). But this community of 78,000, 40 miles southwest of Chicago, has numerous other, more pleasant features. For example, it's known as the City of Spires, for the 122 houses of worship that dot the area.

The temple of art, however, that attracts the cultural faithful from miles around is the old **Rialto Square Theatre,** "The Jewel of Joliet." Built in 1926 by the renowned theater designers, Rapp and Rapp, this masterpiece is a remarkable example of theater baroque. Restored in 1981, it is in the *National Register of Historic Places.* Here, where Fanny Brice and Al Jolson once

35

performed, a list of modern-day luminaries headline the bill at the new performing arts center—Broadway shows, orchestras, singers and comedians.

But in this palace for the people, the real show's before the show. You enter a block-long lobby lined with mirrors, its splendor compared to that of the Hall of Mirrors at Versailles. This lobby leads into the domed rotunda with bas relief sculptures by Eugene Romeo. From the dome hangs the largest hand-cut chandelier in the United States, "The Duchess," 20 feet long with eight arms of copper and bronze and more than 250 lights. Beyond the rotunda is the auditorium, no less impressive. The 21-rank Barton Grande Theatre Pipe Organ is a prized instrument that is used in occasional recitals at the Rialto. Tours are scheduled each Wednesday at 12:45 p.m. or by appointment; (815) 726-7171. Admission, $1. For performance information and tickets, call (815) 726-6600.

The **city's historic districts** are worth inspection, as well. The South East Neighborhood Historic District, south and east of downtown, is a Registered National Landmark District. The feature home is the opulent **Victorian Manor,** a three-story, 40-room Italian Renaissance mansion (at 20 S. Eastern Ave., tours available). Just west of the Des Plaines River, on North Broadway and Hickory streets, are splendid Second Empire-style homes and authentic examples of original Joliet limestone residences. Up the hill from downtown Joliet, west along Western Avenue, are historic old turn-of-the-century Victorian mansions in all of their ornate glory.

Completed for the nation's bicentennial year for a lasting memorial, the **Bicentennial Park Theater and Bandshell** complex at Jefferson and Bluff streets is home to an outdoor concert season and a beautiful 300-seat formal theater. Free weekly lawn concerts are offered each Thursday in June, July and August. Call (815) 740-2216 for more information.

Joliet, named for Louis Joliet, who explored the area with Father Marquette in the 1600s, is home to the county's first junior college. The castellated stone structure, designed by noted architects Daniel Burnham and F. S. Allen in 1902, is today the central campus of **Joliet Township High School** at 201 Jefferson St.

In the city's **Highland Park** is the **Greenhouse**, repository for an exceptional collection of exotic flora. Featured are cacti more than 100 years old and seasonal flower shows.

An essential part of Joliet, as well as Will County as a whole (and Cook, La Salle and Grundy counties), is the Illinois and Michigan Canal. In 1984, it became the newest member of the National Park System, the **Illinois and Michigan Canal National Heritage Corridor**, running from Chicago to Peru, Illinois. It contains historic sites, residential neighborhoods, forest preserves for picnicking, fishing, hiking, canoeing and camping, plus 39 rare natural areas, remnants of the ancient Illinois landscape. Among them is the **Lockport Prairie** at SR 53 and Division Street, south of SR 7, across from Stateville Correctional Center. Some of the best examples of native prairie grasses and wildflowers still may be found there.

Now obsolete, the canal was once the principal transportation link connecting the Chicago and Illinois rivers, providing a continuous waterway from the Atlantic Ocean through the Erie Canal, Great Lakes and the Mississippi to the Gulf of Mexico. The I&M Canal, dug by hand between 1836 and 1848 over 96 miles, made possible the settling of the northern part of the state and the growth of the city of Chicago. Over it traveled immigrants from Sweden, Germany and Ireland, cattle and goods, and the tools of settlement of the American Westward Movement. Settlement and industry followed the opening of the waterway, and with that, the growth of canal towns characterized by distinctive architecture.

One of the most picturesque is Lockport. History in Lockport is everywhere. The town was platted in 1836 by the I&M commissioners to serve as the headquarters for the canal. The headquarters building—in the *National Register* and part of the Lockport National Register Historic District—is now the **Will County Historical Society Museum**—crammed with artifacts of the canal period—at 803 S. State St.; (815) 838-5080. Free. Open daily, 1– 4:30 p.m. from mid-April to September.

Adjacent to the museum is the **Pioneer Settlement**, located along the banks of the canal at Eighth Street. In an open area once used by farmers to load their cargo onto canal boats, the historical society has created an open-air museum with historic buildings brought to the site from around the county. Included are a one-room schoolhouse, a blacksmith shop, a jail and an 1830s log cabin, the oldest building in the county. Open mid-April to September daily. Free.

A 2½-mile **trail** follows the east bank of the canal through Lockport. Accessible year-round by hikers, joggers, bicyclists·

and cross-country skiers, the trail is marked with interpretive signs explaining the history of the waterway. It crosses over old **Lock Number One,** where locally quarried stone walls remain. The trail terminates in **Dellwood Park,** originally built in the early 1900s by the Chicago Interurban Railroad as an amusement park. Today, it boasts tennis courts, a swimming pool, floral gardens, ball fields and a summer program of free concerts at the performing arts center.

A side note: Some of the country's earliest steel plows were first fashioned in Lockport by inventor John Lane in 1835. His plows, which shaped the face of Illinois agriculture, were manufactured at a site near Gougar Road and Seventh Street.

After an afternoon of history, a delightful counterpoint is **Tallgrass,** a decidedly gourmet restaurant, 1006 S. State St., a place that's even been acclaimed by tough Chicago restaurant reviewers. Housed in an 1895 Victorian mansion, the mood is elegant, the food epicurean, the prices steep.

Frankfort, 45 minutes south of Chicago at U.S. 30 and U.S. 45, is known as the "town with 1890 charm." Listed on the Illinois Historic Landmark survey, the **Frankfort Historic District** contains many restored shops and homes typical of a nineteenth-century crossroads village. Today, antique-hunters come from miles around for the village's growing collection of antique shops. Most shops are closed on Monday. The Chamber of Commerce has further information; (815) 469-3356. An annual **fall festival** is scheduled over Labor Day weekend. Visit, too, the **Frankfort Area Historical Society Museum** at Kansas and Hickory streets, open Sunday 1–4 p.m.

In the southern part of the county, Wilmington is one of northern Illinois's most unusual towns. On the Kankakee River, it's known as the "Island City" because the river runs through downtown, forming an island home to two city parks, North and South Island Parks.

Architecturally significant in Wilmington is the **Schutten-Aldrich House,** 600 Water St., a landmark octagonal residence built in 1856. The 1835 **Peter Stewart House** at Kankakee and the Outer Drive, was an important stop on the underground railway in the years before the Civil War.

Catfish Days, held at the beginning of August, is a major tourist event with a Catfish Parade, craft fairs and plenty of fried fish; (815) 476-9841. During the rest of the year, visitors come to Wilmington for the dozens of antique shops in the area.

Nearby, at Braidwood, is the controversial **Braidwood Nuclear Power Plant,** long locked in battle between nuclear critics and its builder, Commonwealth Edison.

The little village of New Lenox is home to two historically important buildings—the red brick **tavern** (now a private residence) on the south side of U.S. 30, just west of the New Lenox–Frankfort border, built prior to 1830 and used as a coach stop and tavern on the Joliet–LaPorte (Indiana) line; and the **Gougar residence** at Gougar Road and U.S. 30, home of the first county postmaster. On the last Saturday in June, the village holds its **Old Campground Festival;** (815) 485-6856.

Off the Beaten Path
in Northwestern Illinois

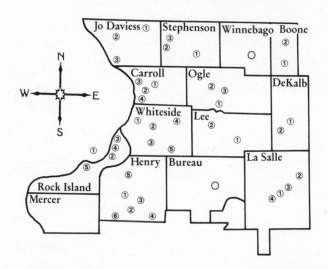

NORTHWEST

Boone
1. Belvidere
2. Capron

Bureau
O Princeton

Carroll
1. Mt. Carroll
2. Oakville
3. Savanna
4. Thomson

DeKalb
1. Dekalb
2. Shabonna

Henry
1. Andover
2. Bishop Hill
3. Cambridge
4. Galva
5. Geneseo
6. Woodhull

Jo Daviess
1. Apple River
2. Galena
3. Hanover

La Salle
1. Naplate
2. Norway
3. Ottawa
4. Utica

Lee
1. Amboy
2. Dixon

Ogle
1. Grand Detour
2. Mt. Morris
3. Oregon

Rock Island
1. Arsenal Island
2. Coal Valley
3. East Moline
4. Moline
5. Rock Island

Stephenson
1. Freeport
2. Kent
3. Lena

Whiteside
1. Fulton
2. Morrison
3. Prophetstown
4. Sterling
5. Tampico

Winnebago
O Rockford

41

Boone County

One of the best ways to see this county is to follow the carefully mapped **Boone County Historical Trail.** Originally compiled by the Boone County Bicentennial Commission and the Boone County Conservation District in 1976, the guide to the trail is available by calling (815) 547-7935.

The trail follows four different routes: the South Prairie Route, running through a region once covered by more than 50 miles of native prairie grasslands; Belvidere/Caledonia Route, covering the county seat, Belvidere and the Scottish settlements at Caledonia and Argyle; Piscasaw Route, which follows the Kishwaukee River and Piscasaw Creek to the Norwegian village of Capron; and the Blaine/State Line Route, beginning at the Kinnikinnick Creek Conservation Acre and traveling through historic Blaine village and across the rolling hills of the Illinois-Wisconsin border. Each route is about 30 miles long, approximating the length of one day's wagon trip in the early settlement days of the 1830s. The trail is designed to be covered by car, on foot by hikers or on bicycles.

The first three routes begin in Belvidere's **Spencer Park,** on the western edge of the city on Lincoln Avenue. Before the arrival of white settlers, this was the permanent gathering place for the local Potawatomi Indians. At nearby **Belvidere Park,** the old **Baltic Mill** dates from 1845 and was in use up until 1918. The fall of water through the Kishwaukee River provided the basic energy to turn the heavy grinding wheel.

At 534 E. Hurlbut Ave. is the former home of one of its early Civil War heroes, **Gen. Stephen A. Hurlbut.** Hurlbut's forces at the Battle of Shiloh won an important victory for the Union, earning him national recognition. He served as a member of the Illinois Constitutional Convention, as a state representative in the Illinois Legislature, as a U.S. Congressman, and as a minister to Columbia and Peru. Hurlbut is buried in Belvidere Cemetery along with dozens of the city's pioneers.

Usually cemeteries are repositories of an area's history, and **Belvidere Cemetery,** at N. Main and Harrison streets, is no exception. Stop at the cemetery office, (815) 547-7642, for a copy of their historic walking tour. Established in 1847, the burial ground holds the graves of two Revolutionary War soldiers, Thomas Hart and Timothy Lewis; the first white woman in the county, Sara Loop; a black soldier in the Civil War and former slave, John Lawson; and blacksmith Samuel

Longcor. Longcor was an early Illinois manufacturer of scouring plows, known as the S. Longcor's Iron Beam, a significant development in the cultivation of the state's prairie lands.

The **Pettit Memorial Chapel,** listed in the *National Register of Historic Places,* was designed by Frank Lloyd Wright in 1907 as a monument to a local physician, Dr. William H. Pettit. The chapel was restored by the Belvidere Junior Women's Club in 1977. It is a fine example of Wright's Prairie School style, with long, low lines. The stucco exterior is painted pale green with dark green wood trim and has a rough sawn cedar shingle roof. Contact the cemetery office (number above) for viewing or a list of open house dates.

Another historic home stands at the corner of Lincoln Avenue and Main Street, the **Col. Joel Walker Home.** The 1840 structure was the residence of a noted hero of the War of 1812.

Big Thunder Park honors the Potawatomi Indian Chief Big Thunder, who died before the first white settlers arrived on the scene in the 1830s. His method of burial, however, provided the town's very first tourist attraction. Following Indian custom, he was buried seated in his best attire, along with food, tobacco and implements necessary in the afterlife, then surrounded by a six-foot-tall log stockade and left to the elements. Early visitors, including travelers on the Chicago-Galena stagecoach who stopped here, were curious and—like tourists today—took souvenirs. Soon, very little was left of Big Thunder. But, undaunted, the local citizenry substituted bones of hogs and sheep, it is said, as relics for the eager and gullible tourists. A boulder with bronze plaque on the grounds of the Boone County Courthouse serves as a memorial.

A greater exploration of local history can be undertaken at the **Boone County Historical Museum,** 311 Whitney Blvd.; (815) 544-8391. Featured are farm implements typical of those that shaped the county's character. The museum is open 2–5 p.m. the third Sunday of every month.

The area's major employer is the **Chrysler Belvidere Plant,** at 3000 W. Chrysler Dr. off U.S. 20 Bypass. Its 4,100 employees turn out Plymouth and Dodge's most popular small cars. During some parts of the year, plant tours can be arranged by appointment. Call (815) 547-2114.

The fall in Belvidere is the time for festivals. The third weekend in September brings **Oktoberfest** to town, with German bands, beer and food, along with carnival rides and craft exhibits. The fourth weekend in September each year, the Boone County Conservation District sponsors the **Autumn Pioneer Festival** with pioneer ethnic gardens, produce samples, volunteers in authentic period dress and an Indian village. Call (815) 547-7935.

Northwest of Belvidere are remnants of the county's immigrant past when Scottish and Scandinavian settlers arrived to take up farming. Caledonia and Argyle (on the Winnebago County line) were, of course, Scottish settlements. In 1834, two Armour brothers and their cousin came to Ottawa, Illinois, from Kintyre, Scotland. Shortly thereafter, they moved to this part of Boone County, which came to be known as Scotch Grove.

Capron, on SR 173 in the northeast part of the county, was home to Norwegian settlers. The first two Norwegian pioneers came to the area in 1842 and called their settlement Helgesaw, later known as Long Prairie.

Bureau County

Great elm trees planted by the founding fathers line the streets of Princeton, a prosperous small town much like it was when it was part of the pioneer path to the west.

Princeton was the home of the abolitionist preacher Owen Lovejoy. Lovejoy, a close friend of Abraham Lincoln, was elected to the State Legislature in 1854 and then to the U.S. House of Representatives in 1856 where he served five terms. Lovejoy became nationally known for his work on behalf of the abolition of slavery. His house was one of the most important stations on the Underground Railway in Illinois. Runaway slaves were hidden here by the Lovejoy family until plans could be made for them to travel to the next station on their way to Canada.

The **Owen Lovejoy Homestead** is now a museum. Listed in the *National Register of Historic Places*, it has 15 rooms and has been restored to reflect the typical furnishings of its era. The home is on U.S. 6 in Princeton. Hours are May through October, Saturday and Sunday 1– 4:30 p.m. For additional information, write Tour Director, 451 S. Main St., Princeton, IL 61356; (815) 875-2184.

Other buildings to look for in Princeton are the **Cyrus Bryant House**, 1110 S. Main St., and the **John Bryant House** at 1518 S.

Main St. Cyrus Bryant's house was built in 1844, and in the front yard is a boulder marking the site of the log cabin that he and his brother John built when they gained the right to buy public land by settling on it.

Another attraction in Princeton is the **red covered-bridge** built in 1863. The bridge is 2½ miles north of Princeton off SR 26.

The second weekend in September is the **Homestead Festival and Annual Pork Barbeque,** complete with an ice cream social, art show, beer garden, street dance, flea market, antique car show, pioneer crafts, horse-drawn wagons and horse show. For information, contact the Princeton Chamber of Commerce, 435 S. Main St., Princeton, IL 61356; (815) 875-2616.

The **Hennepin Canal Parkway State Park**, one mile south of I-80 at SR 88, is a 104-mile waterway with canoeing, boating, hiking and snowmobiling. It was here that engineers discovered how to make water run uphill. The park is open 24 hours a day. Call (815) 454-2328.

Carroll County

Mount Carroll is pure nineteenth-century Midwest America with its cobblestone courthouse square in the center of town, Victorian architecture and 1870s-style storefronts lining Main Street. In fact, Mount Carroll was chosen from among 76 other Illinois towns as a "Main Street, Illinois" town based on the concept of "building on yesterday for tomorrow."

Mount Carroll, located in the northwest corner of the state, about ten miles east of the Mississippi River, was named after Charles Carroll, a Maryland signer of the Declaration of Independence. The town was created by an Act of Legislature in 1839.

Appreciative of its architectural treasures, Mount Carroll has preserved many of its original buildings and a major portion of them are listed in the *National Register of Historic Places.* A self-guided walking tour through the historical sites is available from the Chamber of Commerce, P.O. Box 94, Mount Carroll, IL 61053.

Highlights of the tour include the **Glenview Hotel**, 116 E. Market St., built in 1886 at a cost of $20,000. The hotel remained open until 1976. The lobby is decorated with some of the original

Mount Carroll War Memorial

furniture and a large collection of antiques. The hotel is now an apartment building.

The **Owen P. Miles Home,** located at 107 W. Broadway, has recently been turned into a museum. It is open Sunday afternoons, June through Labor Day, or call (815) 244-8851 for an appointment. It is also open weekdays throughout the year when the curator is in the office.

The Main and Market streets **Commercial Core** architecturally dates back to the 1850s, and a number of buildings were faced with galvanized sheet metal. These decorative facades are said to make up one of the finest collections in the United States.

Inside City Hall, 302 N. Main, the **United States Hissen brass bell,** on loan from the Washington, D.C. Naval Historic Center, is on display.

In the center of the town square is the **War Memorial and Annex,** which is listed in *Ripley's Believe It or Not* as the only memorial with an annex. The annex is to accommodate the 1,284 names listed on the monument. The monument is crowned with a cavalryman designed and sculpted by Lorado Taft, a renowned Midwestern sculptor, lecturer and author.

Mount Carroll holds an annual **Mayfest,** an arts festival and preservation fair, every Memorial Day weekend. Traditional artisans display their wares, showing examples of smithing, glass pottery and performing arts. For a program guide write Mayfest, P.O. Box 94, Mount Carroll, IL 61053; or call (815) 244-9161.

The Campbell Center is a complex of Georgian Revival buildings previously occupied by Frances Shirmer College. The college was established at Mount Carroll in 1853 and closed in 1978. The center was purchased by the Restoration College Association after Shirmer College closed, and the campus now houses the **Campbell Center for Historic Preservation.** The center offers workshops in architectural and fine arts preservations, archeology and the educational, policy and planning aspects of preservation. To contact the Campbell Center call (815) 244-1173 or write: Campbell Center for Historic Preservation, S. College St., Mount Carroll, IL 61053.

The **Oakville County School Museum Complex,** four miles southeast of Mount Carroll, is also nostalgic of the nineteenth-century Midwest. A one-room country schoolhouse, a blacksmith shop and two log cabins are on exhibition. The Carroll County Historical Society operates the complex, and it is open Sunday 2–4 p.m., June 1 through Labor Day and by appointment. Contact the Mount Carroll Chamber of Commerce, P.O. Box 94, Mount Carroll, IL 61053; (815) 244-9161.

Four miles east of Mount Carroll is the **Timber Lake Playhouse,** a live, semiprofessional summer stock theater. The season runs from June 1 to Labor Day and there are evening and matinee performances. New productions are offered every two weeks along with special children's shows. The 425-seat theater is air-conditioned. For information and tickets write Timber Lake Playhouse, P.O. Box 29, Mount Carroll, IL 61053, or phone (815) 244-2035. Tickets should be purchased in advance. For overnight accommodations contact the Mount Carroll Chamber of Commerce; (815) 244-9161.

Moving south along the banks of the Mississippi River is Thomson, home of **Melon Days,** a yearly festival held on Labor Day where watermelon is the star attraction. Thomson has recently restored its **Burlington Railroad Depot** and turned it into a museum, which is open to the public. For information on festival dates and accommodations, write to the Village of Thomson, IL 61285, or call (815) 259-3905.

Mississippi Palisades State Park heads up the natural beauty in Carroll County. The 2,550-acre park is located four miles north of Savanna and is registered as a national landmark by the Department of the Interior. Its location near the confluence of the Apple and the Mississippi rivers gives a breathtaking resemblance to the tree-lined bluffs along the Hudson River in New York, thus the name palisades. Unusual rock formations have been sculpted by water and wind along the cliffs, among them is Indian Head and the Twin Sisters. There are 12 miles of heavily wooded trails for hiking (the back trails giving the best view of the Mississippi), 5 miles of snowmobile trails, 100 acres of open snow area and facilities for picnicking, boating, camping, a playground and nature and equestrian trails. For information, contact Mississippi Palisades State Park, 4577 U.S. 84 North, Savanna, IL 61074; (815) 273-2731. Hours are from sunup to sundown for the park and 7:30 a.m.–midnight for the campground.

DeKalb County

The town of DeKalb can, quite legitimately, claim that it changed the future of the American West. Once known as the "World's Barbed Wire Capital," it was here in 1874 that inventor

Joseph F. Glidden patented an improved method of producing barbed wire. An industry grew up around his invention, with other DeKalb pioneers involved in its manufacture—Jacob Haish and Isaac Ellwood. The **Glidden homestead** and barn at 921 West Lincoln Hwy. is listed in the *National Register of Historic Places.* It's privately owned, however, and not open to the public.

The **Ellwood House Museum,** 509 N. First St., is. This imposing Victorian mansion, appointed with the finest furnishings of the period, is open from April to early December, daily except Monday, 1–3:30 p.m.; (815) 756-4609. Also in Ellwood Park is the Little House, a 10-foot miniature mansion with carefully crafted interiors. The carriage house on the property has a fine collection of buggies and sleighs and samples of, what else? barbed wire. Admission is $2.50 adults; under 12, free.

Northern Illinois University, founded in 1895, is located in DeKalb, as well. The school, with 25,000 enrollment, is the second largest in the state. The architecture of some of the older buildings is worth exploring. Check with the Office of Admissions in Williston Hall for guided tours of the campus and self-guided walking tours; (815) 753-0446. NIU's O'Connell Theater offers performances throughout the year; (815) 753-1635. Admission is free to the anthropology museum in the Stevens Building.

The **Egyptian Theater,** on North Second Street near Lincoln Highway, is a *National Register of Historic Places* building with a unique terra-cotta exterior and excellent acoustics. Built in the Egyptian Revival style, the theater is used for productions by traveling companies and local performing arts groups, as well as for movies; (815) 758-1215.

The 1929 **Haish Memorial Library,** at Oak and N. Third streets, was a gift from another early barbed wire baron. Its art deco Indiana limestone structure, designed by White and Weber of Chicago, was also placed in the *National Register.*

The **Gurler House,** 205 Pine St., is home to a series of special events, such as the **Summers Eve Festival.** The Greek Revival farmhouse, set in a park-like environment, is listed in the *National Register.* Historically speaking, DeKalb also claims the first county farm bureau—in 1912.

Festivals of all kinds are important in the county. Among the most popular are the annual **Sweet Corn Festival** each August in DeKalb (with free corn on the cob); (815) 758-6306.

Sycamore, the county seat, hosts a yearly **Pumpkin Festival** the last weekend in October with pie-eating contests, a bakeoff, and plenty of jack o'lanterns; (815) 895-3456.

Shabbona Lake State Park, in the southwest part of DeKalb County, encompasses 1,550 acres and a 320-acre lake. Fishing is the thing here, and boats can be rented ($30/day for motorboats, $10/day for rowboats) at the marina. While there is no camping yet, hiking trails, horseshoe pits and a baseball diamond are in place. In the winter, there's cross-country skiing, ice fishing and snowmobiling. Write the Site Superintendent, R.R. 1, Box 120, Shabbona, IL 60550; (815) 824-2106.

Henry County

In 1846, a group of idealistic Swedish immigrants came to the Midwest looking for a place to build a communal society. Under the leadership of Erik Janson, a religious zealot, the group founded a commune in **Bishop Hill.** The group, industrious and optimistic, suffered through a harsh winter and epidemics. That year took many of its inhabitants with it. The survivors did establish their version of Utopia, but dissension spread among the ranks and in 1861 the commune dissolved. With the dissolution, Bishop Hill faded into history.

Almost 20 years ago the descendants of the Jansonists decided to restore Bishop Hill. The town is now listed as a National Historic Landmark and as a historic district in the *National Register of Historic Places.* The preserved buildings, located mostly in the center of town, trace the history of the commune.

The **Steeple Building,** once the commune's church, is now a museum. In it craftsmen recreate colony life by demonstrating crafts and other skills practiced by the Jansonists. The museum also has an exhibit of world-famous primitive paintings by Olaf Krans.

The **Bjorklund Hotel,** now restored, is open for visitors but not overnight guests. Both the Steeple Building and the hotel are open daily from 9 a.m.–5 p.m. except holidays.

Numerous shops in Bishop Hill sell antiques, Swedish imports and handicrafts. Local restaurants serve Swedish and American food. For information contact the Bishop Hill Heritage Association, P.O. Box 1853, Bishop Hill, IL 61419; (309) 927-3899.

The **Henry County Historical Museum** is also located in

Bishop Hill, a block south of the town park. Its thousands of artifacts tell of the county's history. Included in its collection are garments, tools, gadgets and furnishings of the late nineteenth century. Five display areas are devoted to special interest subjects, and the exhibits are changed during the season. A nineteenth-century bedroom, a harness shop and a parlor organ are on permanent display. Museum hours are daily from 10 a.m.– 4 p.m., April through November.

The last weekend in September is the **Jordbruksdagarna**— the harvest fest. For specific dates and a list of activities, call the Bishop Hill Heritage Association, (309) 927-3899.

North of Bishop Hill, on U.S. 6 four miles east of Geneseo, is the **Johnson 1910 Farm.** The farm is open for visitors to explore the 130-year-old farmhouse and adjacent buildings. Sights and activities include a little red schoolhouse, old farm machinery, farm animals, costumed guides giving demonstrations and special events on weekends. Or enjoy the timbered picnic areas and hiking trails. The farm is open May 1 to November 1. Hours during June through August are 9 a.m.– 4:30 p.m. daily. In May, September and October, the farm is open on weekends only from 9 a.m.– 4:30 p.m. Admission is $1.50 for adults, $1 for children. Call (309) 944-2040.

Two miles north of Woodhull on Co. Rd. 400N at Co. Rd. 63E is Max Nordeen's **Wheels Museum,** a personal collection of 2,300 items organized around automotive history. The museum is open June through August daily except Mondays and on weekends only in May, September and October. Hours are 9 a.m.– 4 p.m.; (309) 334-2589.

About six miles southeast of Bishop Hill on U.S. 34 is Galva, the sister city to Gavle, Sweden. Galva is the home of **Jacobsen's Home Bakery,** which specializes in rusks, a sweet raised bread toasted until brown and crisp. The rusks are sold in food stores in a 50-mile radius of Galva and are mail ordered around the country.

Jenny Lind, the famous Swedish opera singer, endowed a chapel in Andover, just northwest of Bishop Hill on SR 81. The chapel is open to the public.

The **Henry County Courthouse,** built in 1878–80, is located in Cambridge, the county seat. The main courtroom is worth a look. It is decorated in murals depicting the principal communities in the county.

Henry County has a number of lakes and recreational parks

51

for camping, swimming, fishing, picnicking, hiking, boating and waterskiing. **Johnson Sauk State Park,** off SR 78 four miles south of the Annawan exit of I-80, has 400 acres of campsites along the Old Sauk Trail. **Izaak Walton League Park,** SR 82, 1½ miles north of Geneseo on Hennepin Canal Parkway, has eight acres of camping, fishing, hiking and water sports. The **Circle S Campground** on SR 78 has 80 acres of wooded area and 50 campsites. Circle S is four miles north of the Annawan exit on I-80. The **Timber Campground,** five miles north of Bishop Hill, has 20 campsites with lake swimming, fishing, a pavilion and planned activities. It is located on SR 81, three miles east of Cambridge and one mile north.

Jo Daviess County

Galena is the second largest tourist attraction in Illinois (after Springfield). Although it wouldn't quite be considered "off the beaten path," so many small-town charms are here that it would be a mistake to overlook it.

Galena's life as a tourist attraction began about 20 years ago as a spot to spend the day, browse through a few quaint shops, hunt for antiques and visit the home of Gen. Ulysses S. Grant.

As an introduction to the town, the **Galena/Jo Daviess County History Museum,** 211 S. Bench St., offers two 30-minute self-guided walking tours. This is an excellent way to get your bearings and to decide at which places you will want to spend more time. The tours begin at the Chamber of Commerce office in the railroad depot at 101 Bouthillier St., where you can pick up a map which takes you through the business and shopping district, about six blocks long.

Galena's main attraction is the **Ulysses S. Grant Home.** It's not on the walking tour but is walking distance from the Chamber of Commerce. Instead of heading west across the bridge, go east along Bouthillier Street and you'll run right into it, on the corner of Bouthillier and Fourth streets. The house is open daily from 9 a.m.–5 p.m. and admission is free.

There is also the guided Galena History Tour, which begins at the Galena/Jo Daviess County History Museum on Bench Street. See a slide-tape presentation and tour the museum. Next visit the **General Store Museum,** the historic downtown district and Grant's home.

The tour then travels through **Grant Park** with its statue of the general and recrosses the bridge to end at the 1845 **Market House**, where you see a slide presentation on Galena's architecture.

The tour is $3 per person and includes bus transportation, with an additional $2 charge for the history museum. Contact Sandra Callahan, Galena/Jo Daviess County History Museum, P.O. Box 18, Galena, IL 61036; (815) 777-9129. The museum is open daily 9 a.m.–5 p.m. year-round.

Another interesting stop in Galena is the **Fulton Brewery Market,** just west of the U.S. 20 bridge at the corner of U.S. 20 and Prospect Street. There are 12 retail shops in the building. It is open May 1 through December 31, 9 a.m.–5:30 p.m., January 1 through April 30, 10 a.m.–5 p.m. At 601 S. Prospect St.; (815) 777-1514.

The **Belvedere Tour Home,** Park Avenue, built in 1857, is one of Galena's largest mansions and has been restored and furnished with antiques. Other restored homes that are open to the public are the **John Dowling Stone House,** Diagonal Street; the **Turney House,** U.S. 20 West; the **Old Banking House** and the **Fiddick Tour Home,** Prospect Street. The homes are open 10 a.m.–5 p.m. daily and admission is free.

Galena also has a **House Tours weekend,** the last full weekend in September, when you can view privately owned, restored homes, mansions and cottages not usually available to the public.

An **outdoor antique market** is held Memorial Day weekend and the third Saturday in September on the grounds of the Old Market House. Admission is $2 and you can contact the Chamber of Commerce for information.

The **Old Market House** is open 9 a.m.–noon, 1–5 p.m. daily and admission is free. Inside in the Main Hall are wall panel photos, diagrams and a short narrated slide show about architecture. The South Wing has a commerce and mining exhibit, and the basement has a mural collection of photos and printed documents of the Market House.

On Saturdays from 8–10 a.m., mid-May to late fall, enjoy a farmers' market on the square in front of the building.

The **Grant Hills Antique Auto Museum** has antique, classic and special interest automobiles of yesteryear on display. Hours are 10 a.m.–5 p.m. daily during the summer. No set schedule for the rest of the year, so call (815) 777-2115 for hours.

Galena Cellars, 515 S. Main St., (815) 777-3330, is just inside the Flood Gates on Galena's Main Street in a restored 1840s grainery building.

Galena boasts plenty of places to stay and that includes resorts, hotels and bed and breakfast establishments. The Chamber of Commerce and the Visitors and Convention Bureau have listings. Many of the guest houses and bed and breakfasts are in refurbished homes and are a delightful change from standard hotels.

For additional information you can contact the Chamber of Commerce, 101 Bouthillier St., Galena, IL 61036, (815) 777-0203 or 1-800-892-9299 (1-800-874-9377 for out-of-state calls), or the Convention and Visitors Bureau, 330 N. Bench St., Galena, IL 61036, (815) 777-3557.

The **DeSoto House,** 230 S. Main St., Galena, IL 61036, (815) 777-0090, is a recently refurbished hotel, which originally opened its doors in 1855. The DeSoto House played host to nine presidents, including Abraham Lincoln, and attracted many other famous Americans, such as Mark Twain, Susan B. Anthony and Lorado Taft.

Apple River Canyon State Park has 297 acres for picnicking, camping, fishing, natural hiking and winter sport activities. Contact Apple River Canyon State Park, Apple River, IL 61001; (815) 745-3302. From Warren, drive four miles south on SR 78, then go four miles west on a county road.

The town of Hanover, near Apple River Canyon, has the **Whistling Wings Duck Hatchery,** which raises more than 200,000 mallards every year. This is the world center for mallard duck production. The hatchery is on SR 84, in the middle of town.

In October, the town holds an **Oktober Duck Festival.** The festival is the first weekend in October and is similar to an old-fashioned Oktoberfest. Write to the Hanover Chamber of Commerce, P.O. Box 537, Hanover, IL 61041, or call (815) 591-2201.

La Salle County

Ottawa is a town that remembers its soldiers well. **Washington Park,** in the center of town between Lafayette and La Salle streets, has two war memorials, one dedicated to World War I

Starved Rock Lodge, Starved Rock State Park

and II, Vietnam and Korean veterans, and the other to the county soldiers who fought in the Civil War. The Civil War monument was designed and erected by Edward McInhill, and it lists the names of the soldiers.

The park is a block square and is decorated with flowers and shrubbery. During the summer months an old-fashioned popcorn wagon does business, and piped music plays in the park. Many of the townspeople enjoy their lunch there.

The park also has a boulder for commemorating the first Lincoln-Douglas debate here on Aug. 21, 1858. The memorial was erected by the Illinois Chapter of the Daughters of the American Revolution.

In 1856, Sheriff William Reddick built what is now known as the **Reddick Mansion.** The building is across the street from Washington Park and is listed as a national landmark. It serves as office space for the Ottawa Chamber of Commerce and as a tourist information center. For information visit the building at 100 W. Lafayette St., P.O. Box 888, Ottawa, IL 61350; (815) 433-0084.

The **Third District Appellate Court of Illinois,** just east of the Reddick Mansion, was built in 1857 and served as the State's Supreme Court for a decade. The building is open to visitors during business hours.

Other attractions to see in Ottawa include the statue honoring **W.D. Boyce,** who founded the Boy Scouts of America in 1910. The statue is in the Ottawa Avenue Cemetery, one mile west of downtown Ottawa on Boyce Memorial Drive. Boyce is buried near the statue.

The **Christ Episcopal Church** was the first Episcopal church to hold services in Ottawa in 1838. It is an example of English High Gothic Victorian architecture. The Wallace Window, patterned after a cathedral in Glasgow, Scotland, is a depiction of the Resurrection. It was designed by Professor Julius Herber of Fresden, Germany, one of Germany's finest artists. The church is located at 113 W. Lafayette St.

The **Ottawa Silica Company** office, an example of classic Georgian architecture, is west of downtown on Boyce Memorial Drive.

The old **4978 Locomotive** and weight car was donated to Ottawa by the Chicago, Burlington, and Quincy Railroad in 1966. It is next to the Silica Company office.

The **Ottawa Avenue Memorial Columns** are classic Roman architecture. The columns were built in 1918 as a memorial to Ottawa in honor of the centennial celebration of Illinois statehood. The columns are located next to the Ottawa Avenue Cemetery.

The Ottawa Chamber of Commerce publishes an auto tour of historic sites in the city. Contact them for a copy of the tour: Ottawa Chamber of Commerce, 100 W. Lafayette St., P.O. Box 888, Ottawa, IL, 61350; (815) 433-0084.

The **Starved Rock Land Tour,** also available at the Chamber of Commerce office, begins just outside the Ottawa Avenue Cemetery in the Village of Naplate. The village was named for the former National Plate Glass Company and is now the home of the Libbey-Owens-Ford Glass Company.

The tour continues west through **Buffalo Rock State Park,** named for the rock that resembles a sleeping bison, to the

Half-Way House, once the Sulphur Springs Hotel. The house is privately owned and not open to the public.

The **Grand Village of the Kaskaskia Indians** (1678 to 1700) is the site of three archeological excavations near the Illinois River. Artifacts from the digs are on exhibit at the La Salle County Historical Museum in Utica.

The **Starved Rock Lock and Dam** and **Illinois Waterway Visitors Center** are next on the tour, followed by the **Father Marquette Memorial.**

The **La Salle County Historical Museum** in Utica, just outside Starved Rock State Park, was built during the term of President Zachary Taylor in 1848.

The tour ends at the Visitors Center in **Starved Rock State Park.**

Starved Rock State Park is located ten miles west of Ottawa on SR 71 or south of I-80 on SR 178.

The park's name was derived from an Indian legend, which originated during the 1760s when Pontiac, chief of the Ottawa tribe (which lived upriver from this area), was murdered by an Illinois Indian while attending a tribal council in southern Illinois. Many battles to avenge the death of Pontiac were fought and the Potawatomi tribe, allies of the Ottawas, fought the Illinois Indians in the area called Starved Rock. The Illinois Indians took refuge on top of a butte and were surrounded by the Ottawa and Potawatomi tribes and eventually starved atop the rock.

There is evidence that Archaic Indians as well as the Hopewellian, Woodland and Mississippian tribes lived in the area. Village sites and burial mounds have been mapped by archeologists within the park boundaries.

The largest group of Indians to inhabit the area was the Illinois. They are believed to have lived here from the 1500s to the 1700s. The tribe's population was between 5,000 and 10,000 and was divided into subtribes. The Kaskaskias were a subtribe whose village extended along the north bank of the Illinois River, directly across from the park.

French explorers Louis Joliet and Father Jacques Marquette were the first known Europeans to visit the area. They canoed up the Illinois River from the Mississippi and stopped at the Kaskaskia village. Two years later, Father Marquette founded the Mission of Immaculate Conception, Illinois' first Christian mission, on the site of the Kaskaskia village.

Northwestern Illinois

Rene Robert Cavelier, Sieur de La Salle, came to the area to build a chain of forts to confine the English colonies in the East. Fort St. Louis was built on top of Starved Rock in the winter of 1682–83. It was a strategic post, towering above the rapids of the Illinois River and thereby controlling passage from Canada south. Many Indians settled near the fort for protection from the Iroquois tribe and to be near French trade goods.

In the 1800s there was a movement to make Starved Rock the "Gibraltar of the West," but this plan was unsuccessful. The area was later developed into a vacation spot. In 1911, the State of Illinois purchased Starved Rock and the surrounding area. The park now consists of 2,630 acres and is bordered by a 582-acre nature preserve.

Many interesting rock formations are found in the park; they are primarily of St. Peter's sandstone, laid down by a huge shallow inland sea more than 425 million years ago. It was brought to the surface by an enormous upfold known as the La Salle Anticline. Continual erosion has formed the existing flat surface.

Most of the flat land was glaciated during the past 700,000 years, resulting in a flat and gently rolling plain formed after the last glacier. Most of the prairie is now farmland and the areas along the river are predominantly forest.

There are 18 canyons in the park and these were formed by streams feeding into the Illinois River. The streams cut channels through the rock as they followed the cracks and crevices of the sedimentary layers. Waterfalls are found at the heads of all the canyons, especially after a hard summer rain. The most popular waterfalls are at the St. Louis, French, La Salle and Ottawa canyons.

The park has a wide variety of plant and animal life. Red oak, basswood and sugar maple trees grow in the moist, sandy soil along the northern slopes. Woodchucks feed on the lush undergrowth and moles live on insects found in the soil. Vireos and catbirds fly above the ferns and shrubs. Trillium, Dutchmen's Breeches and the large white flowers of the May Apple tree can be seen in spring.

Along the floodplain, cottonwood, black willows and ash trees grow. Skunk cabbage, marsh marigolds and wild iris live in the marshy areas. Wood ducks nest in hollow trees and can be seen paddling along the river's edge. Beavers and muskrats sometimes appear along the river.

The park has 20 miles of marked hiking tails and hiking information is available at the Visitors Center and park office. The trails are open year-round, but hikers should be cautious near bluffs and stay on official park trails. Metal trail maps are located at all trail access points, trail intersections and points of interest. Colored dots along the trails and on trees assist the hiker; they correspond to letter symbols on trail maps.

Picnicking is permitted and picnic tables, drinking water, toilets, litter cans and metal grills are provided at no charge.

Fishing is permitted but fishermen must stay 600 feet from the dam. Channel catfish are caught between the lock and dam, bullheads from the seawall, white bass from both ends of Plum Island, sauger and walleye from below the dam in fast water, carp from both banks and crappies around the small Leopold Island.

Boats may be launched from the ramp at the west end of the park and canoes are available for rent.

Ice skating is permitted at parking lot C, and cross-country skiing and snowshoeing are allowed in the picnic area and at **Mattiessen State Park** (just southeast of Starved Rock State Park off SR 178). Equipment can be rented on weekends, and tobagganing and sledding is permitted east of parking lot C. Heated washrooms are accessible from these areas. Snowmobiling is not allowed in the park.

The Visitors Center displays the park's cultural and natural history. A park interpreter posts a weekly schedule of activities. The center is usually open on weekend afternoons during peak visitor seasons. If the center is closed, contact the park office, which is open daily from 8 a.m.–4 p.m.

Contact the Visitors Center or Park Interpreter at Starved Rock State Park, Box 116 Utica, IL 61373; (815) 667-4906.

Camping is permitted except in the winter and during the spring thaw. There are 133 sites and permits are obtained at the campground or park office.

There are horseback riding trails and a horseback riders' campground along SR 71 in the far western side of the park. Horse rentals are available on weekends on SR 71, half a mile west of SR 178.

The **Starved Rock Lodge,** inside the state park, is located on a high bluff overlooking the Illinois River. It has 45 rooms and a rustic lounge with a large double fireplace. The lobby is available for public and private use. During the summer months, the Pow-Wow Room in the lodge basement offers refreshments.

Twelve cabins and the Teepee House, adjacent to the lodge, are also for rent. Lodging is available year-round. For reservations and information, call (815) 667-4211 or write Starved Rock Lodge, Schmidt Enterprises, Inc., P.O. Box 471, Utica, IL 61373. Current rates are $42 for lodge rooms with one double bed, $35 for cabin rooms (double occupancy) and $45 for the Teepee House, which includes twin beds.

Norway, 12 miles northeast of Ottawa, is the site of the first permanent settlement of Norwegians in 1834. Inspired by their leader, Cleng Peerson, 14 families purchased a tiny sailing vessel and set sail for America. After the 6,000-mile journey, they founded their colony here.

The Norwegians left home because of economic, political and religious domination by the Swedes. Peerson became known as the Norwegian Daniel Boone because he helped settle the new land in America.

A historical marker on SR 71 commemorates the 100-year anniversary of the settlement and a plaque tells the Norsk Story. The **Norsk Museum,** left from SR 71 on Co. Rd. 2631, is open May through October, Saturday and Sunday from 1–5 p.m.

Lee County

Dixon has gained new stature on the Illinois map as the **boyhood home of President Ronald Reagan.** Reagan lived at 816 S. Hennepin Ave. from 1920 to 1923, from his ninth to twelfth year. Dixonites consider these his formative years. This home is the only family home in Dixon mentioned in the President's autobiography.

After the Republican National Convention in the summer of 1980, a local mailman noticed that the house was for sale. To preserve the house for future generations he put down a $250 deposit and raised the remainder of the down payment through donations. A group of local businessmen signed a note to guarantee the mortgage. The house was purchased for $31,500. Fund-raising activities and donations paid off the balance of the mortgage by the winter of 1981.

The house and adjacent barn are restored to their 1920 condition and although the furnishings are not those of the Reagan family, they are typical of the time period. The refurbishing was completed in time for the president's birthday visit on Feb. 6, 1984.

Listed in the *National Register of Historic Places,* the home is open to the public free of charge. Volunteers act as interpreters and tour guides. Hours are January and February, Sunday from 1– 4 p.m., Monday and Saturday from 10 a.m.–4 p.m. The home is closed Tuesday through Friday. March through December hours are Sunday from 1 p.m.–4 p.m., weekdays 10 a.m.–4 p.m. and closed Tuesday; (815) 288-3404.

Dixon is the petunia capital of the world, and to celebrate, the city holds an annual **Petunia Festival** every Fourth of July weekend. The city boasts that more than 7½ miles of city streets are lined with petunias. The festival also includes a carnival, games, races, performances at the Dixon Theater, a flea market, soap box derby, parade and fireworks. For more information and a schedule of events, contact the Chamber of Commerce, 74 Galena Ave., Dixon, IL 61021; (815) 284-3361.

Dixon is rich in history as its many monuments to nineteenth-century pioneers testify. On the west bank of the Rock River is the site of **Fort Dixon,** built during the Black Hawk Wars. On May 13, 1832, a 23-year-old volunteer marched here from Sangamon County. That volunteer was Abraham Lincoln. The **Lincoln Statue,** a statue of Capt. Abraham Lincoln when he served in the Black Hawk War of 1832, and the **Old Settler's Memorial Log Cabin** are located on Lincoln Statue Drive on the north bank of the Rock River between Abraham Lincoln Bridge and Ronald Reagan Bridge. The cabin is open only during the summer months.

A nearby granite boulder summarizes Lincoln's military services in the summer of 1832 on a bronze tablet in bas-relief. Another bas-relief shows founding father John Dixon with a picture of Fort Dixon and Dixon's ferry and tavern.

The **Nachusa Hotel,** 215 S. Galena Ave., is the hotel of the presidents. Five United States presidents have stayed there: Abraham Lincoln, Ulysses S. Grant, Theodore Roosevelt, William Howard Taft and Ronald Reagan. The hotel was built in 1837 and is the oldest hotel in Illinois. The hotel also claims to have had the first bathtub in Illinois. It is refurbished and the Abraham Lincoln Room is decorated in authentic 1840 decor. The hotel is no longer operating and is not open to the public, but it's worth driving by.

Loveland Community House and Museum, 513 W. Second

St., (815) 284-2741, exhibits local history. Pictures and personal items of John Dixon, a pioneer home, Indian artifacts and a library with county books and records are part of the exhibit. There is also a Reagan memorabilia section. The curator, a classmate of the president, has yearbooks and other souvenirs on display and some personal memories to share. Museum hours are Wednesday, Thursday and Friday 9 a.m.–noon, and the first Saturday of the month 9 a.m.–3 p.m.

Lowell Park, three miles north of Dixon, is a 205-acre park on the Rock River. President Reagan served as a lifeguard here for seven years from 1926 to 1932. On display at the Loveland Community Museum is a plaque, which at the time was affixed to a log on the beach. Reagan notched the log every time he saved a life.

The **Amboy Depot Museum** in Amboy was once the Illinois Central Railroad depot. The 106-year-old building is now a 17-room museum telling the history of Amboy. Museum hours are May 1 through November 1, weekends and holidays 1 p.m.– 4 p.m. Admission is free. No phone, but Amboy is a small community and the museum is easy to find on East Avenue.

Two memorials are near the Amboy depot. One is on the original site of Carson, Pirie Scott and Co. department store, the other is a memorial to the early history of the Reorganized Church of the Latter Day Saints.

Ogle County

Grand Detour is an unincorporated area with about 400 inhabitants, but thousands of tourists visit each year because of a blacksmith named John Deere who opened a shop there in 1836. The shop was the beginning of **Deere and Company,** one of the largest manufacturers of plows in the world.

Grand Detour was named by the Indians because of the oxbow bend in the Rock River at this point. In 1834, pioneer Leonard Andres came to the Rock River Valley and made a claim to the land. He laid out the village of Grand Detour, but, unfortunately, the town was passed over by the railroad and never grew to its early promise of prosperity.

When Deere started farming here, he found that plowing the heavy soil was a difficult job and that most settlers gave up in despair. He experimented with different shapes and materials for plows, and in 1837 he developed a steel plow that worked.

John Deere Historic Site, Grand Detour

Deere and Company is now the oldest major manufacturing business in Illinois and the largest producer of farm implements in the world.

The John Deere Foundation maintains buildings and features of the original property in Grand Detour. An archeological exhibition building covers the site of the original blacksmith shop and displays various machines and how they work. The **John Deere Historic Site** also includes Deere's house, authentically furnished from the 1830s, a visitors center and a blacksmith shop reconstructed on the basis of archeological findings. The shop has a working forge and equipment used by nineteenth-century iron draftsmen.

The John Deere Historic Site is open daily 9 a.m.–5 p.m., March 1 through November 30. Admission is free. For further information, contact the John Deere Historic Site, R.R. 3, Grand Detour, IL 61021; (815) 652-4551.

Other attractions in Ogle County are the **Ogle County Courthouse** in the center of Oregon. The building is listed in the *National Register of Historic Places* and a **Soldier's Monument** designed by Lorado Taft adorns the lawn.

Lowden State Park, across the river from Oregon, is on a bluff overlooking the Rock River. *Black Hawk*, Taft's most famous statue, stands 50 feet high, overlooking the area. Taft and a few artists retreated to this area every summer during the 1920s and created an artists' colony known as **Eagle's Nest.** The public library in Oregon has a collection of works by Taft on display in the second-floor gallery.

White Pines State Forest, eight miles west of Oregon, has 385 acres of recreation and forest area. The lodge has a restaurant, gift shop and lounge. There are also 16 cabins and tent and trailer camping. The park is open from 8 a.m.–sundown year-round, and the lodge is open 8 a.m.–8 p.m. daily, April through October, on weekends only in November and closed the remainder of the year; (815) 946-3717.

Mount Morris, northwest of Oregon, has the **Freedom Bell** dedicated by Ronald Reagan in 1963. The bell was rung in the Illinois Pavilion in the 1964 World's Fair and again at a 1965 Cub's game in Wrigley Field. It is a replica of the Liberty Bell in Philadelphia and is the focal point of the annual **Let Freedom Ring Festival** every Fourth of July in Mount Morris.

Rock Island

Rock Island, one of the Quad Cities, has the Mississippi River as its frontyard and the Rock River as its back. During the 1840s and 1850s, the height of the steamboat era, as many as 1,900 steamboats docked in Rock Island annually.

It was here in 1675 that explorers Marquette and Joliet came on their trip down the Mississippi River. Seven years later they were driven out by the Sauk and Fox tribes. In 1805, Zebulon Pike traveled up the Mississippi on a government inspection trip and found the land inhabited by more than 5,000 Indians.

In 1816, Rock Island was fortified by the government and Col. George Davenport became the first resident-settler. In 1828, other settlers started moving here in large numbers and began battling with the Indians. The Indians retaliated and the settlers sent for help from the governor. They wrote that the Indians, "threaten our lives if we attempt to plant corn, and say that we have stolen their land from them, and they are determined to exterminate us."

The result was the Black Hawk War in which the Sauk and Fox lost their fight, opening up all of northern Illinois for settlement.

The Rock Island Railway, the first to come to the area, completed its railroad bridge in 1855, the first bridge to span the entire Mississippi River.

In 1862 the **Rock Island Arsenal** was built. It originally served as a prison for Confederate soldiers and more than 1,200 prisoners were confined here. When the Civil War ended, the arsenal was converted to its present use as the U.S. Army Armament, Munitions and Chemical Command.

The Rock Island Arsenal was built on what is now known as Arsenal Island, in the middle of the Mississippi River. The arsenal is one of the largest in the world.

The **Clock Tower,** the first permanent building of the Rock Island Arsenal, has a giant clock, over a hundred years old and still running. Visitors can tour the Clock Tower (on weekends and by appointment only) and other sights on the island—a replica of the **Fort Armstrong blockhouse,** the **Court of Patriots Memorial** and a **Confederate Soldier Cemetery.** For tour information contact the Visitors Center at Lock and Dam 15 on Arsenal Island.

Lock and Dam 15 Visitors Center stands above the Mississippi Waterway System, where you can get a great view of barges passing through the lock system. Admission is free. The center is open daily in the summer months 9 a.m.–9 p.m., spring and fall 9 a.m.–5 p.m., winter noon–4 p.m., closed from December 15 to February 3. Call (309) 788-6361 for information about the above mentioned sites and about the Davenport home.

The restored home of **Colonel Davenport** is open for viewing Saturday and Sunday, 1–3 p.m., beginning the first weekend in May through October. It is located on Davenport Drive on Arsenal Island (which was called Rock Island when he settled here, before the town of Rock Island grew in size).

For bikers, an eight-mile **bike trail** around Arsenal Island begins at Terrace Drive at the corner of Gillespie Street.

To reach Arsenal Island, take I-74 in Rock Island, exit at Seventh Avenue, go west to Fourteenth Street. Take Fourteenth Street north to the bridge to the island.

The **Princess Riverland Tours** have daily narrated tram tours of the arsenal. The trams depart from the Seventeenth Street landing at Riverfront in Moline. For schedules and reservations call (309) 324-3287. Tour prices are $6 for adults and $3.50 for children 12 and under.

Rock Island is the site of **Black Hawk State Park,** 1510 Forty-sixth Ave., (309) 788-0177. This is the site of the western-most battle of the Revolutionary War. On the grounds is the **Hauberg Indian Museum** and the **Watch Tower Lodge.** The museum contains a collection of Indian artifacts, paintings and relics. An annual powwow is held on Labor Day. The museum has three rooms, one devoted to Black Hawk items including portraits of the chief, another devoted to the daily lives of the Sauk and Fox, and the third is a gallery of Indian chiefs and the soldiers who opposed them during the Black Hawk War.

The park is open daily from 8 a.m.–10 p.m. and the museum and lodge are open 8:30 a.m.– 4:30 p.m., closed for lunch from noon–1 p.m. Admission is free.

The **Railroad Museum** is where the Old Rock Island Line Depot once was at 3101 Fifth Ave., Rock Island; (309) 788-7200. Its display of railroad memorabilia includes a historic monument noting 100 years of railroading and the first rail crossing the Mississippi River. The museum is open weekends from 9 a.m.–4 p.m. Admission is free.

The **Fryxell Geology Museum,** 639 Thirty-eighth St. on the Augustana College campus, has a collection of fossils, which includes sauropod dinosaur eggs. Admission is free and hours are Monday through Friday 8 a.m.–5 p.m., Saturday and Sunday 1– 4 p.m. Call (309) 794-1318.

The **Denkman Library,** also on campus, has the Augustana Historical Society collection of almost all the Swedish-American newspapers of North America.

The **Genesius Guild,** 1320 Twenty-fourth St., has open air presentations of Shakespeare and Greek classics. Performances run for ten weekends during the summer on Saturday and Sunday. Call (309) 788-9528 for reservations and ticket prices.

Moline has a heritage of Belgian immigrants, and the **Center for Belgian Culture,** 712 Nineteenth Ave., offers demonstrations of Belgian lace being made. Occasionally you can purchase samples. Call (309) 762-0167 for information.

Coal Valley is the home of the Niabi Zoo. Translated from the Indian, Niabi means "Spared of the Hunter's Arrow." The zoo is located on U.S. 6, ten miles southeast of Moline. Besides a variety of animals, the zoo has a miniature railroad and a petting zoo designed for children. It is open April through October, 9:30 a.m.–5 p.m. daily; (309) 799-5107. Admission is $2 for adults, 75 cents for children 4 to 12 years old, and children under 3 are free. Tuesday is free admission for everyone. Rides on the miniature railroad are 50 cents.

Quad Cities Downs is one of the midwest's finest harness racing facilities. Located in East Moline at Morton Drive and SR 5, racing is nightly, Wednesday through Saturday. The track is open from mid-March through mid-November. Post time is 7:45 p.m. every day except Sunday at 1:30 p.m.; (309) 792-0202.

Stephenson County

William "Tutty" Baker, one of the early settlers in Freeport, is responsible for naming the town. Actually it was his wife who teased him about running a "free port" for everyone coming along the trail. Legend has it that one night a group of settlers were discussing a name for the town and Mrs. Baker suggested Freeport because of her husband's generosity.

Freeport is the site of the second Lincoln-Douglas debate, which is marked by a boulder at N. State Avenue and East Douglas Street. The plaque is inscribed with words from both debaters: Lincoln's "This government cannot endure permanently half slave and half free," and Douglas's "I am not for the dissolution of the Union under any circumstances."

The county courthouse, at the junction of U.S. 20 and SR 75, has a **Civil War Monument** which was erected in 1869. On the four corners are life-size figures of a Civil War sailor, militiaman, cavalryman and artilleryman. Engraved on the sides are the names of battles in which Stephenson County volunteers fought. Near the entrance of the courthouse is a plaque commemorating Col. Benjamin Stephenson, Illinois militiaman of 1812.

A bronze statue of Lincoln stands near the entrance to **Taylor's Park,** a mile east of the courthouse on SR 75. **Quality Gardens,** 871 W. Stephenson St., blooms in the latter part of May and early June and is worth a view.

The **Stephenson County Historical Museum** features memorabilia of early social worker Jane Addams, nineteenth-century furnishings and an 1840s log cabin. Part of the museum is a farm exhibit, which displays a typical farm kitchen, a blacksmith shop and many farm machines and tools. A one-room schoolhouse with furnishings dates from approximately 1910.

The museum is located at 1440 S. Carroll Ave., four blocks south of U.S. 20 on Carroll Avenue between Jefferson and Pershing streets. Admission is free; hours are Friday through Sunday 1:30–5 p.m., or by appointment; (815) 232-8419. Closed on holidays.

The **Freeport Art Museum/Arts Council**, at 121 N. Harlem Ave., has a collection of primitive, Oriental and American Indian art, European paintings and sculpture, old and new world antiques, plus a contemporary exhibit. Hours are Wednesday through Sunday and closed holidays. For exhibit information call (815) 235-9755.

Krape Park on Park Boulevard in Freeport is open mid-May through mid-September and has a merry-go-round, flower garden, duck pond, bandshell, boat rentals, tennis courts, playground and concessions. Open daily; admission is free. Call (815) 235-6114.

At the **Kolb-Lena Cheese Factory** in Lena, 3990 N. Sunnyside Rd., (815) 369-5281 (northwest of Freeport), you can watch Camembert cheese being made. The factory, open daily, has a cheesemaking viewing room, lectures on cheesemaking, a cheese shop and tasty free samples.

Lake Le-Aqua-Na State Park, six miles south of the Illinois-Wisconsin state line and three miles north of Lena off SR 73, got its name from the nearby town of Lena and aqua, the Latin word for water. Roadcuts near the park entrance and to the north contain excellent examples of glacial till with varieties of igneous rocks foreign to Illinois. Hours are 6 a.m.–10 p.m. from March 16 to November 14, and 8 a.m.–6 p.m. from November 15 to March 15; (815) 369-4282. Camping, picnicking, fishing, boating, hiking and winter sports are available.

The **Second Battle of Black Hawk** was fought near Kent, and a monument in Kent commemorates the event. The monument is listed in the *National Register of Historic Places,* and every year the town remembers the battle with a celebration. For information contact the County Clerk's Office, 15 N. Galena Ave., Freeport, IL 61032; (815) 235-8289.

Whiteside County

Fulton celebrates its Dutch heritage annually on the first weekend in May. **Dutch Days** are highlighted by *klompen* (wooden shoe) dancing in the streets of town. A parade is preceded by the *burgemeester* (mayor) and the town crier inspecting the streets to see if they are clean. When the major announces that "We must scrub the streets," costumed street cleaners come out with brooms and pails and scrub until the streets are declared clean.

One part of the parade is the "Parade of Provinces," where townspeople wear native costumes from each province of the Netherlands. *Sinterclass,* the Dutch version of Santa Claus, brings up the rear of the parade.

Dutch Delft jewelry and dishes, wooden shoes and authentic costumes are on sale. Local stores offer tastes of Dutch cheese and pastry, and traditional Dutch meals, which include canned beef, potatoes and cabbage, pea soup and currant buns, are served.

The townspeople plant more than 10,000 tulip bulbs every year, and windmills and tulips are in great profusion in Fulton. Even the information booth is housed in a windmill.

During Dutch Days, the town crier walks the street announcing special events, and the library displays Dutch books and shows films of the Netherlands (no admission charged).

The festival ends Sunday afternoon with a traditional Dutch worship at a Fulton church. Men and women sit on opposite sides of the church, and part of the service is conducted in Dutch.

For information, contact Fulton Chamber of Commerce, P.O. Box 253, Fulton, IL 61252; (815) 589-4545.

Tampico is the birthplace of President Ronald Reagan. Born on Feb. 6, 1911, Reagan lived with his family in a six-room apartment above a bakery on Main Street. The **Reagan apartment** is being restored to its 1900s condition but is already open for tours. The downstairs bakery has been converted into a museum and gift shop. Hours are 10–noon, 1–3 p.m., Monday through Saturday, Sunday from noon–3 p.m. Admission is $1 for adults and 50 cents for children; (815) 438-2130.

Prophetstown State Park, in Prophetstown, was once the site of the Winnebago Indian tribal village. The park derives its name from the Indian prophet Wa-bo-kie-shiek (White Cloud). The village was destroyed in the Black Hawk Indian War of 1832. The park borders the Rock River on the northeast side of Prophetstown. Picnicking, fishing and camping are available, but with no lifeguards here, plan on swimming at the city park, just four blocks away. Call (815) 537-2926 for more information about Prophetstown State Park.

Sterling is the location of the **P.W. Dillon Home Museum.** The Italian Renaissance–style brick home at 1005 E. Third St. was built on the 5½-acre lot in 1857. Paul W. Dillon, owner of Northwestern Steel and Wire Co., lived there for 96 years, from his birth in 1883 until his death in 1980. The home has antiques and artifacts on display, and an Engine #73 steam locomotive and caboose. Hours are Tuesday, Thursday and Saturday, 10 a.m.–noon, 1–4 p.m., and Sunday 1–5 p.m.; (815) 625-1078.

The **Sterling–Rock Falls Historical Society Museum** is located in the rehabilitated barn of the Dillon Home. It contains 3,000 square feet of exhibit space for local history. Hours are Saturday 2–4 p.m. and Sunday 2–5 p.m.; (815) 625-1078.

The two **Lincoln historical markers** in Sterling are at 607 E. Third St. and at Sixth Avenue and Sixth Street. A **founder's historical plaque** is at Fourth Street and Broadway, the **Grandon Civic Center** is at Third Avenue, and a **Civil War Monument** and **band shell** are at E. Fourth Street.

Gierhart's Scout Museum, 803 W. Tenth St., displays the complete history of scouting with exhibits and memorabilia. It is open by appointment or by chance, and admission is free. Call (815) 626-0609.

Morrison–Rockwood State Park on SR 78 is located 2½ miles north of Morrison. Lake Carlton, at the center of the park, has a 38-foot-high, 1,800-foot-long dam with a road across it. Fishing, boating, camping, picnicking and hiking are available. Call (815) 772-4708.

The **Old Grist Mill** in Morrison is no longer open to the public but can be seen from U.S. 30 on the west side of Morrison.

Union Grove Cemetery, also on U.S. 30 just outside Morrison, dates back to the early 1800s and is open to the public.

SR 84, running along with west edge of Whiteside County, is part of the Great River Road that parallels the Mississippi River and is one of the most scenic drives in Illinois.

Winnebago County

Time doesn't stand still in Rockford. The **Time Museum,** 7801 E. State St., (815) 398-6000, illustrates the historical development of timekeeping devices from 3000 B.C. to the present. The museum covers the evolution of time measurement from

Stonehenge to the atomic clock, and its world famous collection spans 5,000 years.

The many different kinds of clocks and watches—a total of 3,000 pieces—on display include sundials, astrolabes, nocturnals, compendiums, incense timekeepers, water clocks, sandglasses, calendars, chronometers and navigational instruments.

The Time Museum Bookshop has publications on time measurement and has a variety of art books, children's books, jewelry and souvenirs.

Museum hours are Tuesday through Sunday 10 a.m.–5 p.m., closed Mondays.

Rockford has many museums for those who love browsing. The **Rock Museum Center and Midway Village,** 6799 Guilford Road, Rockford, IL 61107, (815) 397-9112, has a history building featuring local history, an industrial building with 32 local industries represented and Midway Village, a turn-of-the-century village complete with stagecoaches. The village has law offices, a blacksmith shop, an old stone school, a town hall, lumber shops, a jail, a sheriff's office and a bandstand.

The center is open Thursday through Sunday 1–4 p.m. Admission is $1.50 for adults, 50 cents for children under 16. Thursday is free admission day. The center is closed January through the third week of February and holidays.

The **Burpee Museum of Natural History,** 813 Main St., (815) 965-3132 and the **Burpee Art Museum,** 737 N. Main St., (815) 965-3131, are both housed in Victorian mansions. They are open Thursday through Sunday afternoons.

The **Discovery Center** 401 S. Main St., (815) 963-6769, is a "hands-on" participatory museum where you can explore scientific and perceptual principles. The center is open Saturday 11 a.m.–4 p.m., Sunday 1–4 p.m. Summer hours are Wednesday through Sunday 1–4 p.m.

The **Erlander Home Museum,** operated by the Swedish Historical Society, has mementoes of Rockford's rich Swedish history. It is located at 404 S. Third St., (815) 963-5559. Hours are Sunday 2–4 p.m.

The **Graham–Ginestra House,** 1115 S. Main St., (815) 968-6044, is an example of classic Greek Revival and Italianate architecture. It has elaborately painted ceilings and authentic furnishings. It is open 2–4 p.m. the first Sunday of each month, and is listed in the *National Register of Historic Places.*

Rockford also has "The Pride of Rockford," a **double-decker**

tour and charter bus, one of the authentic Bristol Double Decker buses, once part of the national fleet of London. It is available for any type of tour or charter; (815) 968-2232.

Rock Cut State Park, off SR 173 about six miles northeast of Rockford, has picnicking, camping, trails, fishing, boating, ice skating, ice fishing, cross-country skiing and snowmobiling. From Rockford take U.S. 51 to SR 173. For information contact the Site Superintendent, 7318 Harlem Road, Caledonia, IL 61011; (815) 885-3311.

Off the Beaten Path in Eastern Illinois

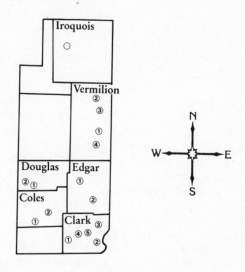

EAST

Clark
1. Casey
2. Darwin
3. Marshall
4. Martinsville
5. Moonshine

Coles
1. Campbell
2. Charleston

Douglas
1. Arcola
2. Arthur

Edgar
1. Palermo
2. Paris

Iroquois
O Gilman

Vermilion
1. Danville
2. Hoopeston
3. Rossville
4. Westview

Champaign County

The 35,000-student **University of Illinois,** the state's largest, shapes the landscape of the twin cities of Champaign/Urbana like nothing else. Lying at the dividing point of the two towns, the university, founded in 1867, is internationally known for its physics and engineering departments. It houses the **National Center of Supercomputing Applications** and is one of only five universities in this country to have a supercomputer on campus (two, in fact). It's a mecca for computer buffs.

Wander around campus and enjoy the architecture or stop at the **Krannert Art Museum,** 500 Peabody Dr., for their collection of sculpture, old masters and the Ewing collection of Malayan art (daily except Monday); call (217) 333-1860. Also on campus is the **World Heritage Museum,** 702 S. Wright, which exhibits the story of man from earliest times to modern day. Open daily except Saturday during the academic year.

Another treasure house, the **Museum of Natural History,** 1301 W. Green, is one of the finest in the Midwest, with thousands of specimens on display. It's the perfect place to take children. Their Discover Room has hands-on exhibits—shells, teeth and other artifacts—that kids can touch and examine closely. Open daily except Sunday. For the lively arts, the **Krannert Center for the Performing Arts,** 500 S. Goodwin Ave., offers a full program of dance, theater and music throughout the year. For schedule information, call (217) 333-6280. Lively sports are represented each season when Illinois meets the Big Ten at **Memorial Stadium,** (217) 333-3470. The university maintains an information desk where they pass out maps and directions at the Illini Union building at Wright and Green streets; (217) 333-4666.

Other sites associated with the University of Illinois are worth a visit, too: The **Morrow Plots** at Gregory near Mathews Street in Urbana are the oldest permanent soil experiment fields in the country, in continuous use since 1876, in keeping with the original agricultural mission of the land grant school. Similarly, three **round dairy barns** built betwen 1902 and 1910 are part of the university's agricultural program (St. Mary's Road, Urbana). Renowned sculptor **Lorado Taft** studied here, graduating in 1879. His student residence, built in 1871, is located at the Illini Grove on Pennsylvania Avenue in Urbana. One of his works, a Lincoln statue, sits opposite Urbana High School on Race Street.

A number of historic buildings are scattered throughout the area. The **Wilbur Mansion,** 709 W. University in Champaign, is a 1907 structure that now houses the **Champaign County Historical Museum.** Open Wednesday through Sunday; (217) 356-1010. Also in Champaign, the **Cattle Bank Building,** 102 N. First, is the oldest remaining business building in the city, incorporated as a branch of the Grand Prairie Bank of Urbana in 1856.

In Mahomet, on SR 47, ten miles west of Champaign/Urbana, **Lake of the Woods County Park** is a pleasant diversion in the Illinois farm country. Here, a 26-acre lake with a sandy beach, fishing and paddleboat rentals attracts families from miles around.

They come, too, for the unique **Early American Museum and Botanical Garden,** located within the park. The museum, opened in 1968, began with the collection of local history buff William Redhead and has grown over the years. Volunteers present a fascinating series of pioneer life programs year-round—from a colonial muster, in September, to an exhibition of farm life a century ago. You might encounter a costumed interpreter making soap or stitching a quilt, dipping candles or spinning a tall folk tale. The demonstration of Christmas past is especially nice during the holidays. For children 5–9 years of age, Wednesday mornings in June and July mean a chance to put on a pioneer costume and spend the time just as a youngster of the 1800s might have, learning antique crafts, games and music.

In the garden, special plantings include the Heritage Garden, the Roses of Yesteryear, the Dye-Plant Garden, and a Prairie Sampler of native prairie plants. An 18-hole golf course, hiking trails plus a covered bridge round out the park's attractions. Call (217) 586-3360 for information. The museum and gardens are open daily from Memorial Day through Labor Day and on weekends during May and September. Hours are 10 a.m.–5 p.m. The park is open daily year-round. Admission charge is $1.50 per vehicle.

Two other parks in the Champaign County Forest District are worth mentioning. **Middlefork River Forest Preserve** near Penfield has year-round camping in addition to three fishing lakes, swimming and an activity center. The preserve is on Co. Rd. 22, about seven miles north of Penfield; (217) 595-5626. **Salt Fork River Forest Preserve** near Homer encompasses the

80-acre Homer Lake, popular with area fishing enthusiasts. The Trailside Visitors Center features nature displays, native animals and an 800-gallon aquarium. In mid-March, the park sponsors **Maple Sugar Days,** a festival of tree tapping, early American crafts, bluegrass music, and pancake sampling (with maple syrup, of course); (217) 896-2455. From I-74, exit at Ogden and proceed south on SR 49 for three miles. Turn right at the sign for the preserve onto Co. Rd. 19. The entrance to the preserve will be in one mile.

At Rantoul, on U.S. 45, **Chanute Air Force Base** is the oldest air training command base in the country, established in 1917. It is one of six technical training centers in the United States where more than 5,000 students a month from all branches of the service enroll in 169 different courses. The base's permanent population is 2,300 military personnel and 1,100 civilians. Visitors must enter through the north gate for the **Chanute Air Park,** an outdoor museum of demonstration aircraft, such as those flown by the Thunderbirds. The park is open dawn to dusk daily. Sixty aircraft are on the ground here at Chanute, and 30 are used as classrooms. At the Display Center, open weekends 9 a.m.–12 p.m. and 1–5 p.m., you can sit in a real flight simulator and learn what pilot training is all about. For information on the base, call (217) 495-4566.

Clark County

Although primarily an agricultural county, Clark County has two literary associations worth noting. James Jones, author of *From Here to Eternity,* was born just south of here, in Robinson, Illinois, and made his home in Marshall, the county seat. Indiana writer Booth Tarkington visited Marshall often as a boy and then recounted those experiences in his nostalgic novel, *Penrod.*

The town of about 4,000 has a wealth of charm that could easily serve as writerly inspiration—quiet streets with leafy canopies of oak and maple, solid turn-of-the-century brick homes. One of the best examples is the 1908 **Lewis Home,** 503 Chestnut, with its dramatic two-story columned verandah (listed in the *National Register of Historic Places,* but not open to public inspection). The old-fashioned bandstand at the county courthouse is home to the oldest continuing city band in the state. The 111-year-old band performs every Friday night on the courthouse lawn from the end of May through August.

Lewis Home, Robinson

The original inhabitants of the county were the Kickapoo Indians, who ceded the land to the United States government in 1819. By 1832, they had been moved from the area. A year later, the site on which Marshall was built was purchased by Col. William Archer and Joseph Duncan, later the sixth governor of Illinois. The town was named after the fourth Chief Justice of the Supreme Court, John Marshall.

Like the eastern states, which are dotted with spots that claim "George Washington slept (or ate or visited or whatever) here," we in Illinois have the Lincoln legend at every turn. The **Lincoln Heritage Trail,** created in 1963, marks the route the family traveled from their original home in Kentucky, through Indiana, to Macon County, Illinois. Here in Clark County, the **Lincoln Trail State Recreation Area** marks the area through which the Lincolns passed in 1830 on their way to a new home in Decatur. The 146-acre Lincoln Trail Lake is its focal point. The park offers camping (electricity, showers and toilets available), fishing (bass, bluegill, crappie, channel catfish), picnicking and hiking on trails up to two miles long. Boats are available for rental. In the winter, enjoy ice fishing, ice skating and cross-country skiing. For information, contact the Site Superinten-

77

dent's office, (217) 826-2222. The recreation area is two miles south of Marshall on SR 1, then drive one mile west.

Mill Creek Park, seven miles northwest of Marshall, is operated by the Clark County Park District, the first county park district to be formed in Illinois (1967). The 2,600-acre park encloses Mill Creek Lake, an 811-acre flood control reservoir. The park opened in 1982. The campground has 139 sites (electric hookups available, no showers). Fees are $6 per night. For reservations, write Clark County Park District, R.R. 2, Marshall, IL 62441; (217) 889-3601. Besides fishing for bass, walleye, catfish, crappie, and bluegill, sample the equestrian or RV trails and the picnicking and swimming areas in the park. Mill Creek Park is on the Lincoln Heritage Trail one mile west of Clarksville.

In Marshall, visit the **Clark County Historical Museum,** 502 S. Front St., built in 1833 as the home of early postmaster Uri Manly. The museum is open free of charge on Sunday 1–4 p.m. during the summer. At the First United Methodist Church, the **Hinners Track Action Pipe Organ** dates from 1909. Find these sights on the walking tour sponsored by the Marshall Area Chamber of Commerce. Write for a brochure, 708 Archer Ave., P.O. Box 263, Marshall, IL 62441; (217) 826-2034. After sightseeing, stop for a hand-dipped ice cream soda at **Martin's Drug Store,** with its now-rare fountain counter.

At what must be one of our favorite-named towns in the whole state, Moonshine, **Moonshine Grocery** is a must-see old country store in the middle of farmland and oil country.

In Martinsville in the west-central part of the county, just off I-70 and U.S. 40 at exit 136, **Newman's Apple House** serves up the fruit fresh from their own orchards—apples, cider, apple butter, along with honey and other goodies. The **Downtown Cafe** is known for its wonderful home cooking. A selection of antique shops make this a worthwhile detour, as well.

At Darwin on the eastern edge of the county, the Wabash River forms the boundary between Illinois and Indiana, and the **Darwin Ferry,** established in 1818, is the only operating ferry in the state.

Casey, on U.S. 40 at Clark County's western border is famous for **Richard's Farm Restaurant.** Situated in an old barn, the specialty of the house is a one-pound pork chop. Enjoy the decor and a seat in the hayloft and perhaps a chat with owners Diane and Gary Richards. Open daily for lunch and dinner;

(217) 932-5300. Dinners range from $8–$13. The restaurant is one block east of the intersection of SR 49 and U.S. 40.

Coles County

The **Lincoln Log Cabin State Historic Site** near Charleston was the last home of Thomas and Sarah Bush Lincoln, Abraham Lincoln's parents. The cabin was built in 1837 and is now reconstructed on an 86-acre lot that includes a pavilion, picnic area and historical farm museum. The cabin is furnished with period pieces, and a kitchen building, log barn and smokehouse from the 1840s have been added to the site. They are being restored to represent New England or "Yankee" culture in Illinois, in contrast to the Lincolns' southern upland culture.

The cabin is open 9 a.m.–5 p.m. daily except holidays, and the park is open 8:30 a.m.–dusk year-round; (217) 345-6489. Costumed guides conduct tours during the summer and admission is free. You'll see signs for it on Fourth Street Road, eight miles south of Charleston.

Fox Ridge State Park is eight miles south of Charleston on SR 130. A wooded tract with rolling hills running along the Embarras River, the park has fishing, boating, hiking, picnicking and camping. For information contact the Park Manager, R.R. 1, Box 234, Charleston, IL 62910; (217) 345-6416.

The **Shiloh Cemetery** is located about 1½ miles southwest of Campbell, along the Lincoln Heritage Trail. Previously called Gordon's Cemetery, it is the resting place of Thomas and Sarah Bush Lincoln. When historians discovered Thomas Lincoln's cabin and began to restore it, the citizens of Coles County dedicated themselves to perpetuating the gravesite. It is also a major cemetery for Civil War veterans.

A few miles north of the Lincoln Cabin on the Lincoln Heritage Trail is the **Moore House** in Campbell. It was the home of Rueben and Matilda Moore. Matilda was the daughter of Sarah Bush Lincoln and was Abraham Lincoln's stepsister. In January, 1861, Lincoln paid his last visit to Coles County and his stepsister at this home. The home is now owned and operated by the state. Open on summer weekends and by request at other times; (217) 345-6489. It is furnished in Civil War–period furniture and other items to give visitors a view of middle-class, pioneer farm life in the early 1860s.

The **Indian Church** is 3½ miles west of Lincoln Heritage Trail between Co. Rds. 1150E and 250N. This was the first church built on the Little Indian Creek in 1832.

The **5-Miles House** at the corner of SR 130 and the Westfield Road (about five miles southeast of Coles County Courthouse in Charleston) was built in 1836. It was originally a wayside tavern and a place to water and care for horses. In 1849, it was an outfitting shop for travelers to the gold fields. It now contains a display of contemporary implements in front of the house (now a private residence).

Greenwood School Museum, at 800 Hayes Ave. on the campus of Eastern Illinois University in Charleston, is the home of the Coles County Historical Society. The building is a restored one-room schoolhouse where local historical items are exhibited. It is open to the public and admission is free. Hours are 1:30–3:30 p.m., Friday, Saturday and Sunday and by arrangement. Call (217) 345-2057.

Eastern Illinois University is the cultural center of Coles County. The battlements of Old Main, an example of German Gothic architecture, tower over the campus. The museum and greenhouses of the Life Science Building are open to the public. Various artworks are on display in the lobby of the Fine Arts Building, and the Paul Sargent Art Gallery is in the Booth Library. The Tarbel Arts Center displays fine art and has changing exhibits. Check with the university for hours; (217) 581-2021. Admission is free.

A replica of the **Liberty Bell** became part of Charleston's heritage during the Bicentennial celebration of 1976. The bell hangs in Morton Park on Lincoln Street (SR 16).

The **Coles County Courthouse,** built in 1898, was remodeled in 1951. Located in Charleston's town square, it is where Lincoln practiced law, and it is the scene of the Charleston Riot, which involved 300 men in an armed conflict during the Civil War.

The fourth Lincoln-Douglas debate was held in Charleston on Sept. 8, 1858. The site of the debate is now the **Coles County Fairgrounds** on SR 316 on the west end of Charleston. There is a display of the debate and six other historic debates, replicas of historic documents relating to the debates and a stone marker commemorating the site.

East of the debate site are the **Old Cemetery** and **Cham-**

bers Cemetery. Here are the graves of Col. and Mrs. Augustus C. Chapman and Mr. and Mrs. Dennis Friend Hanks, relatives of Lincoln. Hanks supposedly taught Lincoln to read and write. There are also graves of many of the early settlers, including Charles Morton, founder of Charleston.

Charleston and Coles County celebrate a variety of festivals. The **1845 Fourth of July Festival** at the Lincoln Log Cabin State Historical Site is a traditional celebration with militia drills, a patriot rally and tug-of-war contest. It is held from 10 a.m.–4 p.m.

In July, Charleston has its **nineteenth-century trade fair.** More than a dozen tradesmen, dressed in period clothing, demonstrate such trades as tinsmithing, blacksmithing, woodworking, tailoring and shoemaking. The weekend of activities is held at the Lincoln Log Cabin State Historical Site from 10 a.m.–5 p.m.

In September, the **1845 Militia Muster** presents a reenactment of early Illlinois militia training with weekend drills, shooting competitions and military inspections. A mock battle is the highlight of Sunday. This is also at the Lincoln Log Cabin site.

For information on the festivals, contact the Charleston Chamber of Commerce, 501 Jackson St., P.O. Box 99, Charleston, IL 61920; (217) 345-7041.

Douglas County

Douglas and its neighboring county, Moultrie, are the center of **Amish culture** in Illinois. The first Amish in Illinois, however, came to the area around Peoria along the Illinois River in the 1830s. These early settlers immigrated from Europe—Alsace and Lorraine, Bavaria and Hesse-Darmstadt. In the succeeding decades, though, Amish from Ohio and Pennsylvania joined those pioneers in Illinois, settling around Arcola and Arthur in the years immediately following the Civil War.

Today, things haven't changed much. You can still see a plainly dressed family riding to town in a black buggy. Indeed, they are called the Plain People, for their belief in life's simple things. They eschew modern conveniences, electricity and stylish clothes. Men dress in black or dark blue suits with "front-fall" pants (sometimes called "barn-door britches"), held up by suspenders. Shirts are of a plain color and style. A flat-crowned,

Amish Country

broad-brimmed black felt hat is worn in winter, exchanged in summer for one of straw. Amish women dress alike in almost every detail, with dresses of a solid color in a pattern handed down over generations. On their heads, they wear a white prayer cap covered by a black bonnet. As you drive down country back roads, you'll find horsepower of the original sort on display—Amish farmers hitched to teams of plow horses. Tractors are not used. Visiting this part of the state is a bit like stepping into a time machine, going back to a time when things were simpler.

One of the best ways to begin a trip here is a stop at **Rockome Gardens,** an amusement park five miles west of Arcola on SR 133. Here, on 12 landscaped acres, nearly everything is constructed of rocks inlaid in cement, everything from fences to arches to garden walls. The Gardens's **Old Bagdad Town** is a recreated frontier village with a general store, bakery, a calico workshop and a gift shop with locally made items from the Rockome Gardens Craft Guild. At the shops, you can find good reproductions of Amish furniture, as well. A popular feature with children is the deer park populated with European fallow deer. Other attractions include a "haunted" barn, a replica of an Amish home and an antique museum. You can get in the spirit of things by taking a buggy ride around the grounds (additional fee).

A schedule of weekend festivals and special events runs all season long—from Horse Farming Days to the Quilt Show to an Old Time Fiddlers' Weekend. **Rockome Family Style Restaurant** serves up Amish-style cooking, including a wonderful shoofly pie. Admission to Rockome Gardens is $5.50 for adults, $4 for children 4–12. The park is open daily from mid-May to mid-October. The gate opens at 9 a.m. and closes at 5 p.m.; (217) 268-4216.

For shopping, the **Arcola Emporium,** at 201 E. Main St. in downtown Arcola, offers the conveniences of a mall with a collection of charming shops selling antiques, art, women's fashions, toys, cookware, gourmet foods and handcrafted solid wood furniture. In addition, a number of fine antique shops are found throughout the region.

The weekend after Labor Day, Arcola hosts the annual **Broom Corn Festival**, recalling the days when it was Broom Corn Capital of the world. A parade, a 10,000-meter road race, a flea market and street fair, plus demonstrations of broom-making, and other old-fashioned crafts highlight the celebrations. For more information, contact the Arcola Chamber of Commerce, Arcola, IL 61910; (217) 268-3841.

Mike Martin, owner of **Po' Ol' Mike's** restaurant in Arcola, claims he serves "warm beer and lousy food," a bit of reverse psychology that packs them in most nights. A graduate of the Culinary Institute, Martin is a professional chef who willingly pokes fun at most restaurants that boast of fine cuisine. Martin's recipe for success is a casual place with specialties such as cornbread, ham, beans, and a tasty beer-battered shrimp. You'll find Po' Ol' Mike's at the intersection of SR 133 and I-57; (217) 268-3812. Most dinners at this popular restaurant are priced under $10.

Edgar County

This may be Illinois's most international county, with a Paris, Scotland, Palermo and even a Kansas within its borders. The county seat, Paris, lies in the heart of a rich farming area. Both Paris and the county date from 1823 when pioneer Samuel Vance donated 26 acres. Today's wonderfully ornate county courthouse (listed in the *National Register of Historic Places*) sits at the center of that land. Vance laid out many of the county's earliest roads, some still traveled today. The county seat gets its name from settlers arriving from Paris, Kentucky, it is believed. Forty years later those southern settlers sympathized with the Confederacy during the Civil War and came to be known as Copperheads. When first established, Edgar County extended north all the way to Lake Michigan. Paris was incorporated as a village in 1849.

A number of historic homes grace this lovely little town. The **Milton K. Alexander Home**, at 130 S. Central Ave., was the residence of a brigadier general in the Illinois Mounted Volunteers during the Black Hawk War of 1832. The house was built in 1826, with additions in 1840. It is now home to the Bicentennial Art Center, open 12–4 p.m. Tuesday through Friday and 1–4 p.m. Saturday and Sunday.

The **Daniel Arthur Home**, 414 N. Main St., was built in 1872 and now houses the Edgar County Historical Society. Open Wednesday through Sunday. For more information, call (217) 463-5305.

Each year in mid-September, the town is abuzz with the excitement of the annual Paris **Homecoming and Honeybee Festival.** Known as the honeybee capital of the nation, the community features its best-known product as well as arts and crafts, an antique car show and a parade. The Honeybee Queen, crowned during the festivities, represents the American Beekeeping Federation throughout the country. Concurrently, the museum sponsors **Prairie Settler Days**—exhibits and demonstrations of pioneer life. Call the Paris Chamber of Commerce for further information, (217) 465-4179.

Twin Lakes Park, the largest of ten in the city, offers camping (tent or RV, toilets, showers, electric hookups), boating, fishing, picnic areas and cooking grills. The star attraction of West Lake is an authentic antique carousel and a small amusement park. The park is on the northern edge of the city on SR 1 and U.S. 50; (217) 465-7601.

Palermo, in the northwest corner of the county, is the site of a historic meeting and peace council between Ottawa Indian Chief Pontiac and George Croghan, the British Deputy Superintendent of Indian Affairs. The 1765 parley settled the uprising known as Pontiac's Conspiracy, which occurred shortly after the French and Indian War.

Iroquois County

Serendipity is prying open an oyster and discovering a pearl. Serendipity, too, is driving through miles of central Illinois farmland and coming upon **The Heartland.** Here in Gilman, this comfortable spa is remarkably unexpected, a Thoreauvian vision of a peaceful retreat some 28 miles from Kankakee down country back roads.

Open just three years, the facility was once the bucolic country estate of Dr. Karl A. Meyer, former medical director of Cook County Hospital. Meyer transformed the farmland, planting 31 acres of woods and creating the manmade Kam Lake. When Chicagoans Gerald S. Kaufman and Charlotte Newberger bought the property in 1983, they decided to preserve much of Dr. Meyer's healthful environment and to expand upon it.

At the edge of the spring-fed lake sits the main house—Meyer's mansion—with accommodations for only 28 guests and a pretty little dining room overlooking the lawn and lake. Here, too, are the Wood Room, where Heartland Institute lectures are held, and the cozy White Room for reading and conversation. An underground passageway leads to the old barn, magically transformed into a three-story fitness center with an aerobics loft, a Cam II gym, sauna, whirlpool, massage and facial rooms. Behind it is an enclosed swimming pool.

Guests begin their stay on Friday or Sunday for either a two-day weekend, a five- or seven-day program. The all-inclusive holiday begins with a tour of the facilities and an orientation, where one of the friendly staff members explains The Heartland fitness and nutrition philosophy. Guests exchange tired big-city clothes for furnished workout togs, the uniform for all occasions throughout the stay. It's all part of the comfortable, casual attitude here.

After an optional body fat evaluation, guests move on to dinner, like all meals a vegetarian affair, beautifully presented and served. Calories are lmited to 1,150 for women and 1,500 for men. Cholesterol, sodium and fats are also limited. But no one goes hungry here. Seconds are okay, if you're not trying to lose weight. In addition to breakfast, lunch and dinner, snacks are available at midmorning and in the afternoon. A fruit basket is always standing ready on the sideboard for those who just can't make it through. One of Chef Morrey Chambers's menus might look like this: minestrone soup, eggplant parmesan, steamed zucchini, fruit garnish, carob coconut cookie. Or for lunch: Waldorf salad, frittata, green beans and almonds.

A day's activities begin early. Wake-up comes at 7 a.m. followed by a morning stretch and a walk before breakfast. After the morning meal is a 1½-hour aerobics class in the fitness center where inhibitions are shed along with pounds, and friendships are formed as guests struggle together through exercise class. By the end of a visit, the spirit of camaraderie is strong, along with the commitment to take home this awareness of healthy living.

Activities, it should be noted, are optional. So at any time, you can wander away for a swim or a hike around the lake, or even a lazy siesta in the sun with a good book. If it sounds like work, it isn't. As Nutrition and Education Director Susan Witz explains, rest and relaxation are among the important benefits of The Heartland, and her presentations, plus those of outside experts, address the issues of dieting and stress.

The Heartland advocates a three-part approach to stress management. The first phase, exercise, focuses on increasing body awareness. Guests explore a variety of exercise techniques. Yoga, guided relaxation and stretching classes increase the participants' awarness of their bodies, using progressive muscle relaxation and controlled breathing.

Education is the second component of the program. Instruction here will help guests become more aware of how tensions accumulate and will introduce various attitudinal approaches, from positive thinking and calming mental imagery to improved communication strategies for defusing harmful stress.

Step three is nutrition, and the spa's balanced vegetarian menus serve that role.

Free round-trip transportation is available from Chicago. For information, contact The Heartland's business office in Chicago, 18 E. Chestnut, Chicago, IL 60611; (312) 266-2050. To reach the spa from Chicago, take the Dan Ryan Expressway south to I-57. Go 52 miles to Kankakee Exit 308. Turn right at the top of the cloverleaf onto U.S. 52/45 (which becomes SR 49) to U.S. 24 (at the flashing red light). Turn right onto U.S.

24 for two miles to The Heartland sign and Camp Wahanaha sign (Co. Rd. 1220E). Turn left and continue for two miles to The Heartland sign. Turn left. The driveway to The Heartland is on the immediate right. The Heartland is 80 miles south of Chicago.

Vermilion County

Illinoisans tend to whiz through Vermilion County and its county seat, Danville, along I-74 en route to Indianapolis and other points east. Why, we haven't really figured out. Besides being the easternmost big city in Illinois (apart from that *really* big one, Chicago), Danville has its charms. Among those are the area's many parks—more than 7,000 acres of parks, in fact, for only 39,000 residents, making this one of the most heavily "parked" cities in the state.

The largest, the 3,000-acre **Kennekuk Cove County Park,** is where the Vermilion County **Civil War Days Festival** is held each year in early June. Hundreds of reenactors from across the country gather in Confederate and Union camps with cannons and cavalry to put on a memorable show. A major antique show and historic craft demonstrations— blacksmithing, candlemaking, spinning, tatting lace— accompany the martial activities. Eighty men and women from the Danville area comprise the **Kickapoo Karvers,** a wood-carving group that's represented at the festival and other area events. Their talent and reasonable prices make them worth seeking out. Kickapoo Karvers, P.O. Box 423, Danville, IL 61834.

Also to be found in the park are four ponds and the 170-acre Lake Mingo, which sounds like something from Flash Gordon. Actually, it's an inviting oasis where Stephen's Beach has all the charm of an old-fashioned swimming hole, replete with a noisy collection of boys and girls. There's fishing in the lake, too—for channel catfish, bass and sunfish.

Follow Lookout Point Trail along a lush ravine system, through meadows and natural prairies. Stop to examine some of the 400 species of wildflowers, plants and trees that grow in the park. Watch for the population of white-tailed deer and dozens of species of birds that are occasional visitors. The park's solar-heated visitor center houses an interpretive display of area Indian history. Kennekuk Cove County Park is eight miles northwest of Danville at Henning Road off U.S. 150. Park hours are 6 a.m.–11 p.m.

What once was an ugly strip mine is today **Kickapoo State Park,** 1,593 acres of woods and fields and ponds popular for picnicking and camping. The Middle Fork of the Vermilion River flows through the park, offering the opportunity for fishing and boating. Half-, one- and two-day canoe trips begin here, with overnight accommodations either at a park campsite or—for the less adventuresome—at a hotel in Danville; (217) 443-4939. Canoes, paddles, and life vests are provided.

State park employees conduct interpretive programs year-round. In the summer they offer guided nature hikes and campfire programs. The park's winter activities include ice fishing, ice skating, cross-country skiing and sledding. Kickapoo State Park is at Exit 210 off I-74. Park hours are 8 a.m.–10 p.m.; (217) 442-4915.

In the southern part of the county, near Georgetown, **Forest Glen Preserve** is unique because of its Beech Grove Handicapped Trail, paved for access by wheelchairs and said to be the only nature trail for the handicapped in the Midwest. It boasts an unusual restored tall grass prairie. Among the park flora, surprisingly, are several varieties of orchids. On I-74, take the Main Street exit right onto SR 150. At the intersection of Main and Gilbert, turn right (south) onto SR 1. Drive into the town of Westville, turn left (east) at the stoplight. The preserve's hours are 7 a.m.–11 p.m.

But, as a major city, Danville has much more to offer than its parks. Its **Civic Center,** built in 1980, is home to entertainment programs year-round, ranging from pop music concerts to ice shows on the center's regulation-size ice hockey rink (also used by the city's professional hockey team and for public skating). The Civic Center is at 100 W. Main St.; call (217) 431-2424 for information.

The **Vermilion County Museum** (116 N. Gilbert, open Tuesday through Saturday 10 a.m.–5 p.m.; Sunday 1–5 p.m.) is housed in a 1850-era two-story brick house, once the home of Dr. William Fithian, a friend of Abraham Lincoln's. Lincoln, in fact, spoke from the balcony while running for U.S. Senate. The local visitor's bureau acknowledges the Lincoln connection with their slogan, "We knew Abe *before* they called him Mr. President." Of special note are the doll collection in the Child's Room and the summer herb garden on the southwest corner of the grounds. Call (217) 442-2922 for information.

The restored **Lamon House** at 1031 N. Logan in Lincoln Park is open to visitors on Sundays, May through October; (217) 442-2922. Built in 1850, it is possibly the oldest frame house extant in Danville. It is furnished with furniture of the period.

With a list of such celebrated native sons as Gene Hackman, Bobby Short, Donald O'Connor and Dick Van Dyke, it's not surprising that the arts scene in Danville is an active one. Community theater, the Danville Light Opera, and the Danville Symphony Orchestra—recently named Illinois Orchestra of the Year—provide cultural sustenance. Call the Danville Area Arts Council for information, (217) 443-3221.

For nourishment of a more basic order, country cooking is the key at **George's Buffet,** 1225 E. Voorhees. From our travels in the state, we've derived the "pick-up quotient" of rating places to eat: the more pickups in the parking lot, the better the food. George's gets a 16-pickup rating. For just $5.50, it's all you can eat, and with hot baked rolls, grandmother-style chicken and noodles and a dozen or more choices, that's a lot of food. Save room for dessert.

In the northern part of the county, Hoopeston and Rossville are good places to look for antiques. Hoopeston hosts the **National Sweetcorn Festival** each September. A beauty pageant, tractor pulls and—of course—plenty of hot corn and butter are hallmarks of this event; (217) 283-7853.

Rossville, on the other hand, calls itself "the village of unusual shops," a very apt description. Along Main Street, shops selling antique furniture, glass, china, primitives and country crafts provide ample fodder for the most ambitious shopping spree. Perhaps the most unusual of these unusual shops is **Aunt Jody's Christmas Bank**, a remarkable display of nativity scenes, angels, nutcrackers and ornaments. Open March through December, most shops closed on Mondays.

Off the Beaten Path in Central Illinois

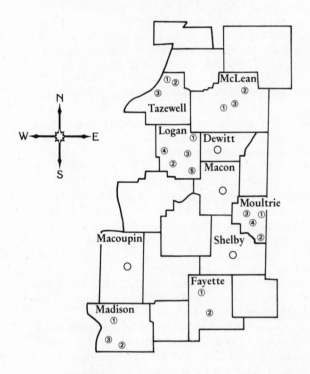

CENTRAL

Dewitt
O Clinton

Fayette
1. Ramsey
2. Vandalia

Logan
1. Atlanta
2. Elkhart
3. Lincoln
4. Middletown
5. Mt. Pulaski

Macon
O

Macoupin
O Carlinville

Madison
1. Alton
2. Collinsville
3. Granite City

McLean
1. Bloomington
2. Lexington
3. Normal

Moultrie
1. Arthur
2. Gays
3. Lovington
4. Sullivan

Shelby
O Shelbyville

Tazewell
1. Creve Coeur
2. East Peoria
3. Pekin

DeWitt County

The center of this county, situated at the center of the state, is **Lake Clinton,** a 5,000-acre cooling lake for the Illinois Power Company's nuclear power plant. With 130 miles of wooded shoreline, the lake development is managed by the Illinois Department of Conservation, which has thoughtfully stocked it with largemouth and smallmouth bass, walleye, crappie and catfish. Sailboats share the lake with fishing boats, which stop for supplies at **Clinton Marina,** off SR 10, about eight miles east of Clinton; (217) 736-2286. In season, hunting is allowed on the land surrounding the lake.

Three miles southeast of Clinton is **Weldon Springs State Recreation Area,** just east of U.S. 51. Prior to 1936, the park was privately owned and the site of a well-known chautauqua each summer. From 1901 to 1920, programs of educational, cultural or religious interest were presented. By 1904, the yearly event drew so many people that it was necessary to build an auditorium accommodating 4,500 people. They came to hear the stars of the day—William Jennings Bryan, President William Howard Taft, Helen Keller, evangelist Billy Sunday and temperance leader Carry Nation, among others. Today, a three-day **Chautauqua Days** celebration is held annually at the end of July with surrey rides, an arts and crafts show, square dancing and plenty of food; (217) 935-2644. The park is open year-round and offers campsites (electric hookups, toilets), picnicking area, hiking trails, fishing and boating. Weldon Springs has a special handicapped-accessible fishing dock, as well.

The **DeWitt County Museum** is located in the **Homestead** in Clinton, a restored Victorian mansion listed in the *National Register of Historic Places.* The 1867 Italianate residence was home to Clinton H. Moore, a former law partner of Abraham Lincoln. The architectural highlight of the structure is a two-story library with vaulted ceiling and an iron railing around the open upper gallery. Children will love the antique doll collection and the child's room with its child-sized four-poster bed. Period rooms, a carriage collection, and the farm and railroad museum are among the exhibits. On the last weekend in September the museum sponsors an **Apple and Pork Festival,** featuring stick-to-the-ribs home cooking with plenty of smoked ham and apple cider. During the Christmas season, the house is beautifully decorated in the style of the late 1800s. The museum is open April through December 1–5 p.m. every day

"The Homestead," Clinton

except Monday, $2 admission. At 219 E. Woodlawn; (217) 935-6066.

A **statue of Lincoln** at the courthouse commemorates the speech delivered in Clinton in 1848 in which Lincoln remarked, "You can fool some of the people all of the time, and all of the people some of the time, but you can't fool all the people all of the time."

Fayette County

Vandalia was the second capital of Illinois, but it was the first capital in the state to build a statehouse from scratch.

The first Illinois statehouse was a rented building in Kaskaskia. It was the seat of state government from 1818 to 1820. When the capital was moved to Vandalia, a two-story frame building was rented and the first session of the Second

General Assembly met here on Dec. 4, 1820. On Dec. 9, 1823, fire destroyed the building.

The State Bank building was remodeled and repaired and became the new statehouse. In spite of the repairs, the building was still in poor condition. It was so unsound that by 1836, no one dared hold a meeting there for fear of the building collapsing.

In August, 1836, Gov. Joseph Duncan authorized Auditor Levi Davis to either have the building repaired, rent an assembly hall or build a new statehouse. It was decided to forget the old plans and build a new statehouse in the style of vernacular Federal architecture.

A bill of $16,378.22 was presented to the legislature for the building. The legislature appropriated $10,378.22 and Duncan drew $5,500 more from the contingency fund. The balance was contributed by individuals. The total cost of the building was $23,241.45.

Some of the important issues discussed at the **Vandalia Statehouse** were slavery and the establishment of Illinois as a free state. The first school laws of Illinois were enacted here and the controversial State Bank was debated here. The city of Chicago was also incorporated by the 1836–37 legislature, which included Stephen A. Douglas and Abraham Lincoln.

As the population shifted, proposals were made to move the capital. On Feb. 18, 1837, the General Assembly voted to move the capital to Springfield.

In 1933, the Illinois Department of Conservation began restoration of the statehouse. At 315 W. Gallatin, it is open daily to visitors from 8:30 a.m.–5 p.m. year-round. Admission is free and guided tours are available. For information call (618) 283-1161.

The area around **Ramsey Lake State Fish and Wildlife Area** was originally called Old Fox Chase Grounds and was popular with fox and racoon hunters. It was first considered as a public recreation area in the late 1920s during the administration of Gov. Len Small. In 1947, the State of Illinois purchased 815 acres for a lake site and additional land acquisition increased the area to 1,880 acres.

Ramsey Lake is one mile northwest of Ramsey, off U.S. 51 in a rolling, wooded terrain. The lake was constructed in a valley with an elevated timbered shoreline of almost four miles.

Ramsey Lake has fishing, hunting, camping, picnicking, hiking, horseback riding and snowmobiling facilities. **White**

Oak Campground has 100 sites with a sanitary disposal station, electric hookups, flush toilets and shower building. Two other campgrounds have more rugged facilities. Reservations are available from the Site Staff.

There are several picnic shelters, which have water, tables and stoves. Fox Knoll, Coon Ridge and Blackberry Fork picnic areas are small, shady, secluded knolls that overlook the lake.

Hikers will find a one-mile designated trail and several miles of unmarked land.

The lake is stocked with largemouth bass, bluegill, redear sunfish, channel catfish and black crappie. Boats can be rented but only electric trolling motors are allowed. Fishing is also allowed in the small ponds. Check with the park office for catch and size limit on fish.

The horse trail is 13 miles long and is at the north end of the area. A small equestrian campground is one mile north of the park entrance.

Dove, squirrel, quail, pheasant and deer hunting are permitted in season, deer hunting only with a bow. Shotguns only are permitted and no hunting is allowed inside of Lake Circle Drive.

Ice fishing, snowmobiling, cross-country skiing, sledding and ice skating are permitted in winter.

For information and reservations contact the Site Superintendent, Ramsey Lake State Fish and Wildlife Area, P.O. Box 97, Ramsey, IL 62080; (618) 423-2215.

Logan County

Local residents say, "Lincoln never lived here but he left a lot of tracks." Abraham Lincoln christened Logan County, owned property here, practiced law at the Eighth Judicial Circuit Court at Mount Pulaski, and his funeral train stopped here.

Logan County was a result of Abraham Lincoln's efforts to divide Sangamon County into four smaller counties in 1839. At his suggestion, one of the counties was named after Dr. John Logan, a friend of Lincoln's who was instrumental in helping persuade the legislature to move the state capital to Springfield.

The town of Lincoln is the only one named with his knowledge and consent. The honor evolved from three partners in Postville, engaging Lincoln as a lawyer to establish joint ownership of the tract of land near Postville. The partners decided to name the town Lincoln, against the advice of Lincoln himself. He said, "Never knew anything named Lincoln that amounted to much."

Walking tours of the town are available from the Greater Lincoln Area Chamber of Commerce, 419 Pulaski St., Lincoln, IL 62656; (217) 735-2385.

The tour begins at the **Lincoln Depot Restaurant**, goes through the **Lincoln House** at 501 Broadway, past the **home of Robert B. Latham,** one of the founders of Lincoln, and past other examples of period architecture. The tour ends at the county courthouse.

The Lincoln Depot and Site is now a restaurant, and on the Lincoln Depot Restaurant's menu is stated: "On August 27, 1853, Abraham Lincoln witnessed the first sale of lots for the new town of Lincoln, named by the town proprietors in his honor. After the lots were sold, Lincoln christened the new community with the juice of a watermelon."

The ceremony took place on or very near the spot where the Lincoln Depot now stands. The Illinois State Historical Society has a sign to this effect.

The Lincoln Depot Restaurant, 101 Chicago St., is open Sunday, 10 a.m.–9 p.m., Monday 11 a.m.–9 p.m., Tuesday through Saturday 11 a.m.–10 p.m.; (217) 735-4433.

Other historical events involving Abraham Lincoln include his and Stephen A. Douglas's visit to the area during their senatorial campaign in the summer of 1858. On Nov. 21, 1860, Lincoln gave a farewell address to the citizens here, and on May 3, 1865, his funeral train was greeted with mourners singing hymns and paying their last respects.

The **Lincoln Gallery,** 111 N. Sangamon, has a statue of Lincoln christening the town. Lloyd Ostendorf's oil paintings depict Lincoln's life in Logan County, Washington, D.C. and Gettysburg. It is inside the Olympia Savings and Loan Association building. Hours are Monday through Thursday 9 a.m.–4 p.m., Friday 9 a.m.–6 p.m. and Saturday 9 a.m.–noon.

Lincoln College was established in 1865 with the donation of ten acres of land by John D. Gillett and Robert B. Latham, two of the founding fathers. The cornerstone of the University Hall was laid on Feb. 12, 1865, Lincoln's last living birthday. The hall is listed in the *National Register of Historic Places.*

The McKinstry Library, on campus, houses the Museum of the Presidents, an outstanding collection of more than 2,500

Lincoln artifacts. The Merrill Gage Statue showing Lincoln as a student is also on campus.

Lincoln Rustic, 412 Pulaski St., is the site where a conspiracy developed to steal Lincoln's body from Oak Ridge Cemetery in Springfield.

The **Postville Courthouse,** 914 Fifth St., is open daily from 9 a.m.–5 p.m., and it was here that Lincoln received his nickname "Honest Abe." The building was completed in 1840 and Lincoln served here as a member of the bar for a quarter of a century. The building was reconstructed in 1953 and the original stands in Greenfield Village, Michigan.

Other sites of interest in Logan County are the **Atlanta Public Library and Museum,** Race Street, Atlanta. The museum contains artifacts from the area, and the building is actually Logan County's first bank. The library is listed in the *National Register of Historic Places* and is one of only a few octagonal-plan libraries in Illinois. Hours are Tuesday through Saturday, 12:30–4:30 p.m.

The **Middletown Stage Coach Inn** in Middletown was established in 1832 and still stands. Middletown is believed to be the oldest town in Logan County and served as a midpoint and stagecoach stop on the Peoria-Springfield Road. The bank building in Middletown is thought to be the oldest building in Logan County.

Elkhart Cemetery in Elkhart has the **John Dean Gillett Memorial Chapel,** a charming country chapel that is privately owned and self-supporting. It was built in 1890 and erected in Memory of John Dean Gillett, the "Cattle King of America."

Richard S. Oglesby, three-time governor of Illinois, is also buried in this cemetery. Oglesby was the person who nominated Lincoln for the presidency and was the first one to call him the "Railsplitter."

Mount Pulaski was named for Count Casimir Pulaski, a Polish-born soldier who joined the Continental army of George Washington in 1777. The **Mount Pulaksi Courthouse** is Greek Revival architecture and one of the two surviving courthouses from Lincoln's days in the Eighth Judicial Circuit court. It is located in the town's square and is open daily from 9 a.m.–5 p.m.

Macon County

Decatur has a cornucopia of architectural styles popular from the Civil War to the Great Depression. Eighty acres of its buildings are listed in the *National Register of Historic Places.* In addition, the Historic and Architectural Sites Commission has published five walking tours, which take you past examples of Italianate, Second Empire, Queen Anne, Romanesque Revival, Shingle, Stick, Georgian Revival, Tudor, art deco and neo-classical styles. The walking tours are free and you can get them from the Decatur Area Convention and Visitors Bureau, 118 Merchant St., Decatur, IL 62632; 1-800-252-3376.

Highlights of the tours include the **Millikin Homestead** at 125 N. Pine, a Victorian mansion with fine woodwork, leaded glass and elegant fireplaces. The **Oglesby Mansion,** 421 W. Williams, is an Italianate-style building with diamond-shaped glass in its bay windows. It was the home of the former United States Senator and three-time governor of Illinois, Richard J. Oglesby.

Abraham Lincoln was no stranger to Decatur. It was here at the 1860 Republican Party Convention that he was unanimously nominated for president and also dubbed the "Railsplitter." A statue of the barefoot Lincoln stands in Lincoln Square in the center of downtown.

The **Scovill Children's Zoo** is a special treat because it is designed to look as if the animals and visitors are in the same environment. The zoo encompasses ten acres and lies above the east shore of Lake Decatur. It is open year-round 10 a.m.–6:30 p.m. in the summer and on weekends, May through October, and 10 a.m.–4 p.m. when school is in session. They have rides on the ZO&O Express and admission is 50 cents for adults, 25 cents for children. Tours are available by advance arrangement.

To get to Scovill Zoo, take U.S. 36 east and cross Lake Decatur to 71 S. Country Club Rd. For information call (217) 224-1712.

The **Macon County Museum Complex,** 5580 N. Ford Rd., prides itself on preserving and presenting the heritage of Macon County. The museum has a collection of historic artifacts as well as examples of 1890s houses, a prairie village and an 1860s schoolhouse. A "hands-on" approach is used in the displays so you can see, smell and touch the past as well as the present. Museum hours are Tuesday through Sunday 1–4 p.m.; (217) 422-4914.

The **Mari–Mann Herb Farm and Gingerbread House** is at the north end of St. Louis Bridge Road. Visitors can walk among the herb beds, wildflower fields, deer trails and formal gardens.

The Gingerbread House offers herb products, Special Spoon Herbal Sauce, herbal jellies and other herbal condiments. Teas, herbs and gourmet spices, fragrances with potpourris, essential and fragrant oils are also sold.

The herb greenhouse carries a selection of year-round herbal plants, homemade candies and herbal breads.

The farm is open 9 a.m.–5 p.m. Monday through Saturday. Demonstrations, luncheons, teas, tours and classes are available by appointment. Contact Mari–Mann Herb Co., Inc., R.R. 4, P.O. Box 7, Decatur, IL 62521; (217) 429-1404.

Decatur is also the home of the **Central Illinois Jazz Festival,** which attracts thousands of jazz musicians and enthusiasts from across the nation. For information call the Holiday Inn, (217) 422-8800.

Macoupin County

Carlinville is home to the **Million Dollar Courthouse,** more affectionately termed the "White Elephant." The courthouse was far beyond the needs of the county and cost much more than anticipated when construction began in 1867. Within a few months, the building commissioners and the county court knew that the building would be more than double the $150,000 estimated cost.

It took 2½ years before the building was finished and 40 years before it was paid for. When it was finally completed, the move from the old courthouse to the new was quietly made. The eventual cost was $1,300,000.

The building is made of limestone and consists of two rectangles that cross at the center and are surmounted with a dome. The dome rises 191 feet above the street and 40-foot columns support the roof. Every door is made of iron and each outer door weighs more than a ton. All the interior trim is of iron or stone. The judge's chair, costing $1,500, is mounted on a track behind the varicolored marble bench.

Macoupin County Historical Museum has a collection of county historical items, a music room with an old grand piano, exhibits of furniture, pottery, china and glass, stained glass windows from a German exhibitor at the 1893 World's Fair in Chicago, an 1890 bathroom and memorabilia of early Macoupin County doctors.

A gift shop on the premises carries postcards, county history reprints and craft items. Hours are April through November, Wednesday 10 a.m.–2 p.m., June through August, Sunday 1–5 p.m. Admission is $1.50 for adults and children over 16; 50 cents for 6–16-year-olds, no charge for children under 6. The museum is on Breckenridge Road in Carlinville; (618) 635-3489.

Madison County

Alton was the site of **Alton Prison,** the state's first penitentiary. The remnants of a cell block wall have been restored as a monument to this primitive penitentiary, which housed Confederate prisoners during the Civil War. The monument is at the corner of Broadway and Williams streets near downtown Alton.

The town's colorful history includes Rev. Elijah P. Lovejoy, a newspaperman who crusaded against slavery and was shot down by a hostile mob. Lovejoy was shot on Nov. 8, 1837, and 60 years later, a 90-foot stone memorial was erected near his grave. In 1915, the frame of his printing press went on display in the lobby of the Alton Telegraph Building.

Looking for more pleasant sites in Madison County, you'll find the **Lewis and Clark State Park,** south of Wood River on SR 3, two miles north of I-270. The park commemorates the starting point of the famous expedition to the Pacific Coast. The monument to the expedition consists of 11 concrete pylons, which form the rotunda, and represent the 11 Trail States traversed by the expedition. Individual plaques briefly review the party's activities as it traveled cross country.

The **Cahokia Mounds** in Collinsville are a world heritage site. The site has changed from a camping, picnic and playground facility into a valuable international cultural resource. The site and Museum Society offer educational programs and publications. There is also a gift and book shop. Take I-55/70 to Exit 11 at SR 157, then south to U.S. 40, then west to Cahokia Mounds World Heritage Site.

The main feature are the 65 intact mounds. Originally there were approximately 120 mounds and most were ceremonial. Monk's Mound is the largest prehistoric mound north of Mexico. The mounds are open daily from 9 a.m.–5 p.m. except on major holidays.

Horseshoe Lake State Park on SR 111, west of Edwardsville, is on a low floodplain, which follows the Mississippi River down to the Kentucky border. The lake was formed as a result of heavy spring floods causing the river to overflow its banks and cutting new channels through the bottomlands. During this process, an old river section was cut off from the flowing channel forming a natural oxbow lake. Horseshoe Lake was formed in this manner.

The area was inhabited by Indian groups, the earliest evidence from 8000 B.C. during the Archaic Period. Artifacts have been found that fall into the Woodland Period, 1000 B.C. to 1000 A.D.

The park has picnicking, playground equipment, fishing, camping, hunting, four miles of hiking trails and three miles of cross-country skiing. The park is open year-round except for holidays. Contact the Site Superintendent, Horseshoe Lake State Park, P.O. Box 1307, Granite City, IL 62040; (618) 931-0270.

McLean County

At the heart of the Illinois prairie sit the sister cities of Bloomington and Normal. The earliest records show the first white men in the county around 1800—traders and trappers who made a living roaming the region bordering the Mississippi River. A local legend says that one such group hid a keg of whiskey here in a thick grove of trees, only to have it discovered by an Indian party that finished it off handily. Thus, when the first settlers arrived in 1822, the place was called Keg Grove. Seven years later, when the first post office was established, the settlement called itself Blooming Grove for the area's profusion of flowers.

McLean County was organized in 1830 and a year later, Bloomington, laid out on 22½ acres donated by James Allin just north of Blooming Grove, was designated county seat. Normal, once North Bloomington, takes its name from what was the State Normal University, now Illinois State University (founded in 1857). Bloomington's university, Illinois Wesleyan, was chartered in 1853. Apart from being university towns and a center of county government, the communities have a rich business and industrial base. For example, the home office of State Farm Insurance Company is based here.

History and politics have long been intertwined here, as well. Some say Bloomington's David Davis was the man who "made Lincoln president." A noted lawyer and member of the state

Ewing Manor, Bloomington

legislature, Davis was elected judge of the Eighth Judicial Circuit in 1848, a position that put him in frequent contact with the lawyer Abraham Lincoln. At the 1860 Republican Convention, Davis worked behind the scenes to organize support for Illinois's favorite son. In 1862, Lincoln rewarded him with an appointment to the Supreme Court. Davis was elected to the U.S. Senate in 1877.

His mansion, **Clover Lawn,** is one of the top attractions for visitors. A state historic site, the 20-room Italian villa includes much of the original furnishings from the 1872 period. The house is built of yellow face brick with stone quoins in the corners. Its tower rises 50 feet above the ground. Inside, eight marble fireplaces decorate rooms done in high Victorian style, a fine example of upper-class life of the period. Free one-hour tours are available Thursday through Monday 9 a.m.–4 p.m., 1000 E. Monroe, Bloomington; (309) 828-1084.

Another mansion *cum* museum is the **Ewing Manor**—also known as Ewing Castle—**Cultural Center**. The former home of Hazel Buck Ewing, whose father was associated with William Wrigley, Jr., in the foundation of the Wrigley Company of Chicago, the 1929 estate is done in the style of a Norman castle. Upon the death of the wealthy philanthropist, the property became part of the Illinois State University Foundation, open to the public as a cultural center and Museum of Nations. It houses the school's collection of African, Oceanic, and pre-Columbian art and the International Collection of Children's Art.

The galleries are open free to the public by appointment on Tuesdays and Thursdays 12:30–4:30 p.m., for groups of 10–30. Emerson Street at Towanda Avenue; (309) 438-8800. Tours of the home can be arranged by appointment, Monday through Friday 10:30 a.m.–4:30 p.m. for groups of 8–30; (309) 829-6333.

In July and August, the **Illinois Shakespeare Festival** presents three Shakespearean plays here in repertory nightly Tuesday through Sunday. Before the performance, the **Illinois State Madrigal Singers** entertain. Picnicking on the lawn of the Ewing Manor is especially popular with festival-goers; (309) 438-2535.

The **McLean County Historical Society Museum** catalogues the county's past with exhibits of Indian artifacts, decorative arts, military souvenirs and crafts. Special shows are mounted throughout the year. One of the star attractions is the "Tilbury Flash," a 1930s racing plane built in Bloomington, among the smallest in the world. Tours are conducted daily from 1–5 p.m., 201 E. Grove St., Bloomington; (309) 827-0428.

The **Miller-Davis Museum,** 101 N. Main St., Bloomington, houses exhibits commemorating early attorneys, merchants and builders. The 1840s Federal-style building was used as a temporary office by Abraham Lincoln while riding the judicial circuit. Today, it's part of the county historical society's holdings. Tours are available Tuesday, Thursday and Saturday noon–3 p.m.; (309) 829-2132.

Illinois State University provides plenty to keep a visitor busy. Stop at the university art galleries, the Funk Gem and Mineral Museum, the planetarium, the Hudelson Museum of Agriculture, or the school's historical museum. The Adlai E. Stevenson Memorial Room honors one of Bloomington's most famous citizens. And there really is an academic ivory tower here—Watterson Towers, at 28 stories the world's largest college residence hall. Most campus attractions are free and tours can be arranged. Call (309) 438-8800 for ISU information. Regular performing arts events are scheduled at Braden Auditorium, call (309) 438-2222 for schedules.

Illinois Wesleyan, too, boasts a number of treasures including Evelyn Chapel, a focal point of the private school. The chapel is an example of Moravian-style architecture in Flemish bond patterned brick. The interior woodwork and acoustics are superb. Sheean Library holds the Indian pottery collection of Maj. John Wesley Powell, a former faculty member and first explorer of the Colorado River and Grand Canyon. Call (309) 556-3031 for campus information. McPherson Theater has a busy schedule of productions throughout the year; (309) 556-3232.

Bloomington's **Miller Park Zoo**, 1020 S. Morris Ave., is one of Illinois's best. The Tropical Rain Forest, 80 feet in diameter, has overhead skylights, a profusion of tropical plants and colorful exotic birds flying free through the exhibit. Outside, the antics of the California sea lions or the American river otters captivate crowds. The James E. Gardner Memorial Children's Zoo features farmyard animals for kids to pet. The zoo is open every day of the year, in the summer from 10 a.m.–7 p.m.; the rest of the year 10 a.m.–5 p.m. Free admission on weekdays beginning December through first of March. At other times: adults, 75 cents; 3–17 years, 35 cents; (309) 829-7961.

A major seasonal event is Bloomington's **American Passion Play.** Since 1924, community players have enacted the life of Christ in an annual spring tradition with a cast of 350. Sundays, mid-March to early May at the Scottish Rite Temple, 110 E. Mulberry St. Tickets, $7.50–8; (309) 829-3903.

At 901 N. McLean in Bloomington is the site of the **Adlai E. Stevenson I home.** Stevenson was vice president of the United States from 1893–97. Both he and his grandson, Adlai Stevenson II, former governor of Illinois, are buried at Evergreen Cemetery here. Another Illinois governor—this one a Republican—lived in Bloomington, as well. **Joseph W. Fifer,** governor of Illinois from 1889–93, lived at 909 N. McLean, near the Stevensons. Both homes are privately owned and not open for tours.

One of the area's most unusual tours is offered at **Funk Seeds International,** U.S. 51 South in Bloomington. The hour walking tour takes you through the working area of a commercial seed conditioning plant. Tours by appointment Monday through Friday, 8 a.m.–3:30 p.m.; (309) 829-9461.

Southwest of the county's two major cities is historic **Funks Grove.** One of the county's first settlements, several of the original buildings still remain—the **Funk Prairie Home, chapel** and **syrup factory.** To reach Funks Grove, take I-55 south to the Shirley exit; the town is about ten miles southwest of Bloomington. Hours by appointment, call (309) 827-6792.

Five miles west of Bloomington on Co. Rd. 1650 North, **The Apple Barn** sells jams, cider and fruit from McLean County's oldest commercial orchard. Open daily, July through December (except Sundays in July); (309) 963-5557.

In Lexington, northeast of the major cities, stands the **Patton Cabin,** built in 1829 by John Patton, one of the county's first white settlers.

For campers, **Moraine View State Park,** near rural LeRoy, offers 1,700 acres of rolling terrain plus the 160-acre Dawson Lake. Boating, fishing, camping (142 sites, most with electrical hookup) and hiking are popular activities. Call (309) 724-8032.

Moultrie County

While farming may be the primary economic enterprise in Moultrie County, fishing is probably the primary pastime. Sullivan, the county seat, advertises itself as the "northern gateway to beautiful **Lake Shelbyville.**" It shares the 11,100-acre lake with Shelby County to the south. So at the same time the county claims first place in statewide corn-per-acre production, its production of walleye, crappie and largemouth bass isn't bad either.

If you're camping, try **Fox Harbor Campground and Marina,** south of town on Lake Shelbyville; (217) 728-7312. There's boat and canoe rental and plenty of wooded terrain just across from the **Sullivan Recreation Area,** which has a well-maintained swimming beach.

Sullivan is situated on the Lincoln Heritage Trail, as well. It claims to be the only town with a National Guard unit once commanded by Abraham Lincoln. Less honorably, it was also the scene of a near-riot on the day that both Lincoln and Douglas were in town to give speeches.

The **Little Theatre on the Square** is the town's pride and joy and Sullivan's claim to summer cultural fame. Founded in 1957, it bills itself as the only professional Equity theater between Chicago and St. Louis. And each year from the end of May through mid-August, a program of musicals and plays is presented with performers of some repute; (217) 728-7375.

The town square with its historic domed courthouse is the perfect spot for an evening stroll after supper, which, of course, would be taken at **K-Zel's**, 8 W. Harrison, a family diner that's everyman's ideal of country cooking, right down to the mashed potatoes and gravy. Fried chicken is on the "don't miss" list, along with breakfast—biscuits and sausage gravy, eggs and heavenly hot cakes. Prices are inexpensive and the restaurant is open 24 hours a day.

On the north side of town, **Wyman Park** and **Wyman Lake** make up 40 acres of recreational area offering tennis, a playground and room for picnicking. Nearby, the **Civic Center** has an Olympic-size indoor heated pool with diving area, racquetball courts and a gymnasium.

Just outside of town, east on SR 121, is the **Illinois Masonic Home.** Land for the home was given before the century by Mason Robert A. Miller upon which to build a residence for Masons and their widows. The first building was dedicated in 1904. Today, more than 300 retired persons reside here. Its beautiful grounds include a deer park, a landscaped lake and a greenhouse that furnishes fresh flowers daily for the home. A small collection called **Ward's Museum** is housed in the main building. Open to the public, it includes 10,000 specimens of seashells, plus primitive furniture and other antiques. In a separate building is an old-fashioned ice cream parlor complete with a marvelous player piano. Visitors are welcome at the home year-round; (217) 728-4394. Hours are 8 a.m.–4:30 p.m. Monday through Friday, 8 a.m.–4 p.m. Saturday and Sunday. No admission charge.

Also outside of town is **The Depot,** on Co. Rd. 3 six miles west of Sullivan, an antique store housed in the old Chicago and Eastern Illinois railroad depot; (217) 797-6351. Hours are 9 a.m.–4 p.m. Monday through Saturday. If you can't make it out to the country, however, they have a gallery in Sullivan at 1015 W. Jackson.

But in the country, stop at any one of the numerous farm stands for fresh produce. For example, you can pick your own strawberries in season at **Lewis Schlabach**'s on SR 133, five miles west of Arthur, and five miles north of the Masonic Home.

Surprisingly, the county has the distinction of housing two sites featured in Ripely's *Believe It or Not*—the **Flag House** east of Lovington on SR 133, and the amusing **two-story outhouse** at Gays on SR 16.

Shelby County

Shelby County is blessed with natural resources set aside for public recreation. Within its boundaries lie Hidden Springs, Wolf Creek and Eagle Creek state parks; Lake Mattoon; Lake Pana; and—most importantly—**Lake Shelbyville.** This giant lake is one of the state's largest, covering 11,100 acres, with 172 miles of wooded shoreline protected from development by the U.S. Army Corps of Engineers. It reaches 20 miles from Shelbyville, the county seat in the south, to Sullivan in Moultrie County in the north.

Begun in 1963 and completed in 1970 as a flood control project, the lake contains the Kaskaskia and Okaw rivers. Today, the recreational benefits are primary on the minds of most visitors with camping, boating, fishing, picnicking, hiking and swimming all available to weekend adventurers. Call (217) 774-2020 for recorded lake fishing conditions. Your catch might be white or largemouth bass, walleye, crappie, channel catfish, northern pike or any one of two dozen or so varieties of fish found in the lake.

There are only three marinas on the lake—**Fox Harbor** in Moultrie County and **Lithia Springs** and **Findlay** in Shelby County. Lithia Springs is closest to Shelbyville and boasts a modest motel, the **Lithia Resort,** only a short walk away. An alternative accommodation choice, however, is offered in house-boat rental. Lithia rents 35- and 43-foot houseboats by the week or portion of a week for prices ranging around $300–$800; (217) 774-4121. For that, you can bring six or eight people and make it a party. To reach Lithia Springs Marina, drive three miles east of Shelbyville on SR 16, then turn north and follow the signs.

Sailboats and fishing boats, water-skiers and naturalists happily coexist on the lake where deep forested coves seem far away from the flat farmland not too distant. On shore, campers will find more than 500 campsites with electrical hookups. During the summer season, Corps of Engineer personnel present a schedule of interpretive programs on a range of spiffy topics: "Family Water Safety," "Through an Insect's Eye," "Wild Edible Plants," and others. Be sure to stop at the Visitor Center at the Dam East Recreation Area, one mile east of Shelbyville on SR 16 (open Memorial Day through Labor Day), which offers audio-visual programs, exhibits and an unmatched view of the dam.

Apart from the lake, there's plenty to see ashore. In Shelbyville, named for Revolutionary War Gen. Isaac Shelby, drive up Washington Street to view the handsome Civil War-era homes. Downtown, the French Second Empire-style county courthouse is a local point of interest. The old, multisided **Chautauqua Auditorium** in Forest Park dates from the period around .1903 when evangelist Jasper L. Douthit held his celebrated religious meetings here. Today, country-western music brings in the faithful each summer week.

Tazewell County

Pekin, once a major port on the Illinois River during the steamboat era, is one of the oldest settlements in the county. Like many other towns in western Illinois, it was visited by Abraham Lincoln and was used as a fort during the Black Hawk War.

Pekin, too, is the home of the **Everett McKinley Dirksen Congressional Leadership Center,** the nation's only educational institution devoted to the study of congressional leadership. The center is located at Broadway and Fourth streets. It contains the late senator's office files, speeches, audio and visual tapes, records, photographs, books and memorabilia. The major exhibit is "Congress: The Voice of the People." This exhibit shows examples of how the citizenry participates in the legislative process.

In addition to the Exhibition Hall, the center has a growing collection of memorabilia relating to Congress. Senator Dirksen began the collection with contributions of his own artwork, sculpture, photographs, flags, letters and political mementos. These objects are used in special exhibits.

Visitors can tour the Exhibition Hall and also view special programs offered in the Assembly Room. These programs must be arranged by advance request. Admission is free and the museum is open to the public Monday through Friday 9 a.m.–5 p.m. Additional winter hours are Saturday 10 a.m.–4 p.m., September through May; (309) 347-7113.

The Pekin area lies at the boundary between the Bloomington Ridge Plain that was formed by Wisconsin glaciers nearly 22,000 years ago and the Springfield Plain formed by Illinoian glaciers about 200,000 years ago. The geological history of the Mississippi and Illinois rivers can be studied through **field trips** sponsored by the Illinois Department of Energy and Natural Resources, State Geological Survey Division, Natural Resources Building, 615 E. Peabody Dr., Champaign, IL 61820. Call (217) 344-1481 for information.

In mid-September, Pekin holds its **Annual Marigold Festival** to celebrate the flower, which blooms throughout the city. A parade and art fair are part of the celebration. Contact the Pekin Chamber of Commerce, 116 S. Capitol, P.O. Box 636, Pekin, IL 61554, (309) 346-2106, for a list of activities.

The **Spring Lake State Conservation Area,** one mile south of Pekin on SR 29, nine miles southwest on Manito Blacktop, and three miles west on Spring Lake Blacktop, is a 1,996-acre park with a fish hatchery, fishing, boating, hiking, hunting, cross-country skiing and picnicking facilities. Contact the Park Manager, R.R. 1, Box 248, Manito, IL 61546, (309) 968-7135, for information.

East Peoria, at the base of the bluffs on the flood plain of the Illinois River, is the home of **McGlothlin Farm Park.** Located on Neumann Drive off Meadows Avenue at U.S. 150, the park is a picture of farm life. It has duck ponds, a schoolhouse, barn, brooder, blacksmith shop and hen house. Animals on the farm are typical of those on many area farms and are free to roam the grounds. Visitors are allowed to pet and feed them. For information call (309) 694-2195.

The **General Store**, on the grounds of the park, offers a variety of toys, country items and candy. The **Country Kitchen** is open to view antiques, and, when a special event is scheduled, baked goods are baked in an old wood stove on the premises. Concessions as well as picnic tables are available. Hours are 9 a.m.–6 p.m. Tuesday through Friday, 11 a.m.–6 p.m. Saturday and 1–6 p.m. Sunday. Admission is 75 cents for adults, 50 cents for children.

Fon du Lac Park at Springfield and Steward avenues in East Peoria has an extensive view of Peoria and the Illinois River Valley. Its more than 2,000 acres on the east bank of the Illinois River offer picnic areas, hiking, golf, tennis, camping and swimming facilities. Call (309) 699-3923.

Fort Creve Coeur State Park in Creve Coeur was once the site of explorer La Salle's outpost. The fort, established in 1680, was ill-fated. It was a proposed base for exploration and colonization of the Mississippi Valley, but when La Salle went to Quebec and left another man in charge, the dissatisfied troops destroyed the fort and went into the wilderness with all the powder and provisions. The fort was never rebuilt. A granite marker commemorates the founding of the fort and tells the story of its desertion.

The **Fort Creve Coeur Rendezvous** is an annual event held the fourth weekend in September. The festivities feature voyageurs with canoes, buckskin-garbed troops, flintlocks and crafts. Contact Fort Creve Coeur State Park for dates and information at (309) 694-3193.

Off the Beaten Path in Western Illinois

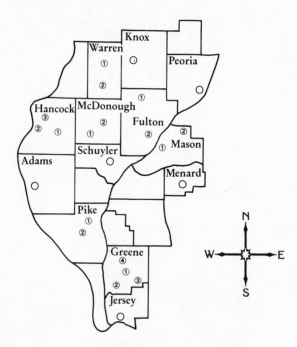

WEST

Adams
O Quincy

Fulton
1. Ellisville
2. Lewiston

Greene
1. Carrollton
2. Eldred
3. Kane
4. Whitehall

Hancock
1. Carthage
2. Hamilton
3. Navoo

Jersey
O Grafton

Knox
O Galesburg

Mason
1. Havanna
2. Manito

McDonough
1. Colchester
2. Macomb

Menard
O Petersburg

Peoria
O Peoria

Pike
1. Griggville
2. Pittsfield

Schuyler
O Rushville

Warren
1. Monmouth
2. Roseville

Adams County

The most impressive feature of Quincy, a rivertown on the east bank of the Mississippi River, is its architecture. Stately mansions and fine old commercial buildings of Italianate, Greek Revival, Romanesque, Queen Anne, Prairie and Moorish designs fill the town.

The **John Wood Mansion**, 425 S. Twelfth St., is an example of Greek Revival architecture. The home was built in 1835 by the founder of Quincy and former governor of Illinois, John Wood. Take an escorted tour of the restored home and see the audio-visual presentation. The **Osage Orangerie Gift Shop** is on the premises and offers handcrafted items reminiscent of the early nineteenth century.

The 14-room mansion is listed in the *National Register of Historic Places*. It was originally located across Twelfth Street, but Wood had the house moved to its present site in 1864.

On display are furnishings and many personal items of the Wood family as well as objects recalling Adams County's history. Included are a Victorian dollhouse, the first piano in Quincy, Quincy-made stoves, a table used by Abraham Lincoln, a chandelier from a Mississippi River steamboat and a sunstone from the Mormon Temple in Nauvoo.

Museum hours are 1–4 p.m. Saturday and Sunday. Other times by appointment. Admission is $2 for adults, $1 for students; (217) 222-1835.

The **Newcomb-Stillwell Mansion** is now the home of the **Quincy Museum of Natural History and Art.** The home, built in 1891, is listed in the *National Register of Historic Places*. The exterior has leafy carved ornamentation and window transom bars of solid stone. Building materials of contrasting colors and textures enhance its bold facade and forceful design. It is an example of American architectural standards of the 1800s.

The museum exhibits a collection of Indian relics, clothing, weapons and accessories. There are also African safari trophies and a large collection of fossils, seashells and butterflies.

In the special discovery area, children can touch museum objects and learn through observation and creative activities. A miniature circus for children, the work of the late Milton Kalmer of Quincy, contains virtually every element of an old-fashioned circus—tiny circus animals, clowns, acrobats, a train, a band with musical instruments and circus-goers in the stands.

Governor John Wood Mansion, Quincy

The museum is located at 1601 Maine St., Quincy, IL 62301; (217) 224-7669. Hours are weekends and by appointment only. Guided tours are available. Admission is $2 for adults, 50 cents for students and free for children under five.

The **Villa Katherine,** 532 Gardner Expressway, (217) 223-1000, is a Moorish-style castle. It is located on a bluff overlooking the Mississippi River and is listed in the *National Register of Historic Places.* The building is under restoration but is open to the public. Tours are available by appointment and admission is $1 for adults, 50 cents for students.

The **Quincy Art Center** is located on the grounds of the **Lorenzo Bull Home,** 1515 Jersey St., and is open to the public. The Carriage House was designed by Joseph Lyman Silsbee, a prominent Chicago architect and mentor of Frank Lloyd Wright. The center contains a permanent collection of paintings, sculpture, graphics and a library of art books and periodicals. It also has temporary and traveling exhibits.

Hours are 1–4 p.m. Tuesday through Friday, 2–5 p.m. Saturday and Sunday. Admission is $1 for adults, free for students; (217) 223-5900.

Quincy has a number of museums that are worth visiting. The **Quinsippi Island Antique Auto Museum** is located in Quincy's All-American Park on the banks of the Mississippi River. Sixty-five antique cars and related displays make up the exhibit. The museum's collection includes a 1917 Chevrolet Royal Mail Roadster, a 1911 Little, a St. Louis–built Diana, a 1901 Columbia Electric, a Ford Roadster pickup featured in television's "Hee Haw" and a horse-drawn hearse.

The museum is located at Front and Cedar streets; (217) 223-4846. Hours are 11 a.m.–5 p.m. Sunday and by appointment. Admission is $1 for adults, 12 and under 50 cents. The group rate is 75 cents.

The **Gardner Museum of Architecture and Design** is in the Old Public Library Building built in 1888. At Fourth and Maine streets it is open from 1–5 p.m., Saturday and Sunday. The museum contains stained glass windows from Quincy churches, photographs and examples of terra-cotta, metal, fine woodwork and other ornamentation from early Quincy homes. Admission is $1 for adults, 50 cents for seniors and students; (217) 224-6873.

All Wars Museum, 1701 N. Twelfth St., (217) 222-8641, displays military memorabilia with a military library and films. It is on the grounds of the **Illinois Veterans Home,** one of the nation's largest.

Hours are 9–11 a.m., 1–4 p.m. Saturday and Sunday; Wednesday, Thursday and Friday 1–4 p.m. It is open holidays and admission is free.

The **Pharmacy Museum of Quincy and Adams County** is located at Fifth and Chestnut streets. This century-old former drugstore has pharmaceutical artifacts and apothecary items. It also displays antique soft drink trays, postcards, and an Edison Victrola playing vintage music. Hours are 1–4 p.m. Saturday and Sunday or by appointment. Admission is free; (217) 224-1000.

The **Lincoln-Douglas Valentine Museum,** 101 N. Fourth St., (217) 224-3355, has a unique collection of old and unusual valentines on exhibit. It is open 10 a.m.–2 p.m. Monday through Friday. Admission is free.

Quincy's public square at the center of the uptown historical district was originally called John's Square, honoring the United States president for whom both Adams County and Quincy were named. The square became **Washington Square** in 1857. One year later it was the site of the sixth senatorial debate between Lincoln and Douglas. The spot is marked by a commemorative plaque sculpted by Lorado Taft in 1935.

The **Clot Adams General Store** at 200 Front St. was once a favorite haunt of rivermen, and it is still open to the public. The **Quincy Levee** has steamboats for moonlight excursions and runs daily trips to Hannibal, Missouri, in the summer. Several warehouses and buildings along the levee are from the steamboat era.

Riverview Park on the northeast corner of Quincy, overlooking the Mississippi River, has a statue of George Rogers Clark. This was the site of the Black Hawk War skirmish in Quincy. In **Woodland Cemetery**, South Fifth Street, is a Soldier's Monument dedicated to Adams County men killed in the Civil War, along with the grave of John Wood.

Quincy celebrates its **Annual Dogwood Festival** the first week in May. Festivities include a parade, crafts fair and military band concert along with the sight of all the dogwood trees in bloom. For a list of events and times contact the Quincy Chamber of Commerce; (217) 222-7980.

Fulton County

If old bones, skulls and Indian burial grounds grab your interest, Fulton County is the place you should visit. It is one of the richest archeological areas in the Midwest. There are 800 mounds in Fulton centered around the junction of the Spoon and Illinois rivers. The most famous is the **Dickson Mound** near Lewiston.

The Dickson Mound is on a high bluff overlooking the two rivers. It was originally crescent-shaped with the points facing east. It measures 550 feet along its outer curve and 35 feet high. A reproduction of one of the burials is exhibited at the Field Museum of Natural History in Chicago.

A museum adjacent to the mound has the largest display of its kind in the country, exhibiting more than 200 skeletons. It is one of the few on-site archeological museums in the Midwest.

The museum's collection includes remains and artifacts displayed in their original position when found, pottery, vessels, mussel-shell spoons, el-shaped pipes, bone needles, beads, stone adze blades and effigy forms.

A colored-light display highlights the ghostly features of Indian skeletons, and maps and cases explain the Mississippian Indian culture of 1000 B.C.

Down the hill from the museum is a reconstructed village of the same period.

The mound is located off SR 97 and SR 78 near Havana, five miles south of Lewiston. Museum hours are 8:30 a.m.–5 p.m. daily and closed on holidays. The gift shop and coffee shop are closed from mid-December to April 1. Grounds are open to dusk from May 1 to November 1. Admission is free; (309) 547-3721.

For the literary-minded, Edgar Lee Masters immortalized the **Spoon River Country** and particularly Lewiston in his *Spoon River Anthology*. Masters's home was in Lewiston and Oak Hill Cemetery on North Main Street shows many names identical to characters in the anthology. The area is also filled with interesting buildings, historic markers and antique shops.

The **Ross Mansion**, 409 E. Milton Ave., was the inspiration for the McNeely Mansion in the anthology. The mansion was modeled after a home on the Hudson River that Col. Lewis W. Ross admired. The New England–style home has 17 rooms and is made of stone from the Spoon River Valley.

Major Newton Walker's house had the honor of having had Abraham Lincoln as a guest. The home was built in 1833 and is located at 1127 N. Main St. Unfortunately, it is not open to the public.

Other places of interest in Lewiston are the **Phelps Store,** Main and Washington streets (originally an Indian trading post) and the **Church of St. James** at Broadway and Illinois streets, an example of Victorian Gothic architecture.

In the neaby town of Ellisville is an **opera house** from the nineteenth century, and in London Mills is the **Ross Hotel**, an authentically restored hotel.

The **Spoon River Scenic Drive** takes you through 60 miles of woodland and towns. To obtain a map from the Spoon River Scenic Drive Associates, write to them at Box 59, Ellisville, IL 61431, or call (309) 293-2143. Also, signs mark the drive.

The first two weekends in October are the **Annual Spoon River Festival.** Contact the Spoon River Scenic Drive Associates for information.

Greene County

This county lies in the west-central part of the state on the Illinois River, about 20 miles from its mouth. Primarily an agricultural region, the terrain is marked by broken, hilly land at its western edge along the river bluffs. Here, fruit cultivation is an important industry.

A number of historic sites are found throughout the county: In Carrollton, the county seat, the **Hodges Building** on the northwest corner of the town square houses the Greene County Historical Society. The **County Courthouse,** along with the entire square, is listed in the *National Register of Historic Places.* On the west side of the town square is the former home of **Major Marcus Reno,** who fought with Custer in the Battle of Little Big Horn.

The **Henry T. Rainey Home** is one-half mile east of Carrollton on SR 108. The three-story brick house faced with columns holds a wealth of historical artifacts. Rainey was the Speaker of the House in the 73rd Congress. In **Rainey Memorial Park,** on the north edge of town, a bronze statue honors the legislator who served in every session except one from 1903 until his death in 1934.

One of the few working farm vacations in the state can be had at **Hobson's Bluffdale Farm,** four miles north of Eldred on the Bluff blacktop road. It's good old-fashioned fun with plenty of outdoor activity. The farm holiday includes lodging, truly memorable meals, horseback riding, hayrides and swimming. The 1828 **John Russell House** is situated on the property, as well. For reservations. call (217) 983-2854.

Other recreational opportunities are available at **Greenfield Lake,** 1½ miles east of Greenfield; and **Roodhouse Reservoir,** two miles east of Roodhouse. Both offer camping, fishing and boating. But, of course, the Illinois River is the major body of water in these parts. Try waterskiing downstream or take a free ferry from the terminus of SR 108, west of Eldred, across to Calhoun County.

For golfers, there is the **Lone Oak Golf Course,** three miles east of Carrollton on SR 108, then right 1¼ miles on the country road. The nine-hole course is situated in a beautiful rural setting; (217) 942-6166.

In Whitehall, in the northern part of the county, the **Annie Louise Keller Memorial** is a sculpture by the famous artist,

Lorado Taft, dedicated to a schoolteacher who lost her life rescuing her pupils during a tornado in 1927. Here, too, is the grave of the Little Drummer Boy of Shiloh.

Plan a drive along the river bluffs from Eldred to Hillview. It's especially pretty in the fall. In the southeast corner of the county, at Kane, **Nila's Country Kitchen** serves up country cooking at its best; (217) 942-6135. Prices range from $3–$6.

Hancock County

Hancock County, at the western edge of the state where the Mississippi turns and bends its way around Illinois's bulging middle, has a rich and colorful history inextricably linked with the Mormon religion. It was here, at Nauvoo and Carthage, that some of the most significant—and tragic—chapters of the Mormon history were written.

What was once the site of Sauk and Fox Indian villages, by the 1830s had come to be a sleepy river village known as Commerce. After being driven out of Missouri in the spring of 1839, church founder Joseph Smith brought his followers here, to the place he called Nauvoo, to create a homeland for his people. By special negotiation with the Illinois Legislature, the group obtained a charter that allowed them extraordinary powers—their own courts, militia, university—and any other authority not prohibited by the United States or Illinois constitutions. Nauvoo became virtually an autonomous state. With Mormon converts arriving from across the country and from overseas, the town grew to be Illinois's largest, with 8,000 homes and a population of 15,000 by 1842.

Discontent with the leaders' power grew within and outside of the church. When a group of dissidents published an anti-establishment newspaper with views critical of the leadership, the paper was destroyed. For that, Joseph Smith and his brother, Hyrum, were jailed at the county seat, Carthage. An anti-Mormon mob stormed the jail and murdered the churchmen. Brigham Young took control of the group and, in 1846, led them west to Utah.

Nauvoo was abandoned until 1849, when a group of French communalists, the Icarians, arrived from Texas to practice their own brand of philosophy under their leader, Etienne Cabet. Their experiment lasted until 1856. During their tenancy, however, they began the production of wine and cheese, which continues today.

Today, groups associated with branches of the Mormon church have extensively restored Nauvoo and the old Carthage jail. The **Nauvoo Restoration Visitor Center** at Young and Partridge streets includes a historical exhibit and a short film on the early days of the community. Admission is free. Hours are 8 a.m.–8 p.m. in the summer and 8 a.m.–7 p.m. in the winter; (217) 453-2237. Just outside the center is a sculpture garden, the **Monument to Women.**

Some of the historic homes and shops open to visit in Nauvoo are the **Brigham Young Home;** the **Mormon newspaper office** of the *Times and Seasons;* the **Joseph Smith Mansion; Jonathan Browning's gunsmith shop;** and the **Clark store**. Many have guides and period craft demonstrations. The historic homes are open from 9 a.m.–6 p.m. in the summer and from 9 a.m.–5 p.m. in the winter.

On the hill overlooking the river plain where the temple community grew are the ruins of Smith's **Great Temple**. The **Nauvoo Chamber of Commerce Tourist Reception Center,** on SR 96 in the center of town, has a self-guided cassette tape tour and maps of the area available. Open daily 9 a.m.–4:30 p.m. April through October; (217) 453-6648.

Nearby, the **Nauvoo State Park** features a museum operated by the Nauvoo Historical Society, with a 100-year-old vineyard and wine cellar. Camping, a playground, picnic area and a stocked fishing lake are also available at the park. For more information, contact the Site Superintendent, Nauvoo State Park, P.O. Box 337, Nauvoo, IL 62354; (217) 453-2512.

Labor Day weekend marks the annual **Nauvoo Grape Festival,** (217) 453-6600, with tastings of the local blue cheese and wine. Throughout the year, some delightful tastes come from the kitchen of the **Hotel Nauvoo.** The hotel, once a private home, dates from the Mormon period around 1840. In addition to the restaurant, where dinner prices range from $7–$14, there are a limited number of overnight accommodations; a double costs $35–$45. At 1290 Mulholland; (217) 453-2211.

In Carthage, the **old jail,** which once held Joseph and Hyrum Smith, is open for free tours daily from 9 a.m.–7 p.m., 307 Walnut St.; (217) 357-2989.

Also of interest is the **Hancock County Courthouse,** a Greek Revival structure that's one of the prettiest in the state. It was here, on Oct. 22, 1858, that Abraham Lincoln addressed a crowd of 6,000 in his senatorial campaign against Stephen A. Douglas. A stone marker commemorates the event.

The **Show 'n Tell Museum,** 417 N. Madison, is an ideal place to take children. A 13-room house dating from the 1890s, the museum is overflowing with teddy bears (more than 700 of the furry creatures); dolls (more than 200); dollhouses and miniature rooms. Open daily by appointment, $2 per person; (217) 357-3456.

The **Dr. Alice L. Kibbe Museum,** at U.S. 136 and Scofield Street, is the personal collection and home of a former biology professor at the now-closed Carthage College. The collection includes Civil War relics, Indian artifacts, fossils and rocks, and a natural history exhibit. Open daily 1–4 p.m. Memorial Day through Labor Day or by appointment. Free. Call (217) 357-3119.

Along with western edge of the county, the Great River Road runs next to the Mississippi, providing dramatic views and scenic photographic opportunities. In the winter months, from early November through early March, bald eagles roost in the vicinity. January is the best time for observation around the open waters below Lock and Dam No. 19 near Hamilton. From sunrise to around 10 a.m. is the best time to catch the eagles feeding. The **Alice Kibbe Life Science Field Station** of Western Illinois University on the Hamilton-Warsaw Road is open for nature observation and hiking at most times of the year. Emory Carson, resident manager of the station, is available by appointment from 9 a.m.–5 p.m. to explain the eagle's natural environment. Call (217) 256-4519.

Jersey County

Father Jacques Marquette, a French Jesuit missionary, and explorer Louis Joliet were the first Europeans to come to this area in 1673. The history of the area, however, is traceable back some 200 million years when movements of the earth resulted in dislocation of rocks, producing the Lincoln Fold in Pere Marquette State Park.

Pere Marquette State Park lies five miles west of Grafton on SR 100 in Jersey County. It is an 8,000-acre park lying on bluffs that overlook the confluence of the Mississippi and Illinois rivers.

Another trace of prehistoric times is McAdam's Peak, where twin springs flow from Ordovician-Silurian rocks that were deposited in the sea 350 million years ago. All the ridges have loess (pronounced less) on them. Loess is wind-blown dust laid down a million years ago during the Great Ice Age. The river's banks of yellow clay are composed of loess and capped with black topsoil that supports the forest.

Prehistoric man also left his mark here. There are 18 sites indicating his presence, and a village once stood where the park lodge now stands. Nomadic hunters and fishermen lived in the Illinois valley about the beginning of the Christian era and Stone Age men left remnants of arrowheads and coarse, heavy pottery.

When the French came to this region, the tribes of Illinois, Potawatomi and Kickapoo Indians remained near their ancestral cemeteries and burial mounds. Their houses and village sites dotted the Illinois Valley and are still visible throughout the park.

The **Pere Marquette Lodge,** located in the park, (618) 786-3351, is scheduled for reconstruction beginning in the fall of 1986. Call the lodge for an update on construction. Currently the lodge has 18 rooms with air-conditioning and heating plus seven stone guest houses. There is a dining room, and a 700-ton stone fireplace is in the lobby. The park also has what is believed to be the world's largest chess set. The board is 12 feet square and has figures bigger than the average six-year-old.

Within the grounds is an amphitheater with a movie screen. The theater seats about 200 people. There are also facilities for boating, camping, fishing and picnicking, and more than 15 miles of hiking trails and horseback riding.

The Visitors Center displays the history of the park, and a park interpreter is available for assisting bus tours, hikes, demonstrations and talks to large groups. For reservations with the interpreter, call (618) 786-3323 or write Park Interpreter, Pere Marquette State Park, Box 325, Grafton, IL 62037.

Knox County

Galesburg is a city that retains the flavor of the nineteenth century through its architecture. The city is so proud of its treasures that it published six walking tours, 30 to 45 minutes each, that take you through the historic districts, pointing out buildings and telling tales of Galesburg's history. The tours are available through the Illinois Department of Tourism or from Galesburg Chamber of Commerce, 154 E. Simmons St., Galesburg, IL 61401; (309) 343-6409.

Carl Sandburg Birthplace, Galesburg

In the mid 1830s, George Washington Gale, Galesburg's founding father, came to the area to create a labor collective similar to Oneida Institute of Science and Industry, a collective he founded on the east coast. Galesburg began as a religious colony under Gale's leadership, and in June, 1836, 560 acres were allocated for the town and 104 acres for a college. By the end of the first year, 40 families were established in Galesburg.

Railroads were the mainstay of the town. In 1854, the first train, called *Reindeer*, came to Galesburg. The railroads allowed for area produce to be shipped to other markets and employed a major portion of the town's work force. By 1880 the town had quadrupled in size and grew in prosperity as evidenced by the many large Victorian homes here.

Galesburg's public square was the starting point for commerce in the town. The first general store was established at the northwest corner of Broad and Main streets. The square was traversed by trolley tracks and was proposed as the site of the courthouse or post office. But, after 140 years, the square still remains an open, grassy area.

Galesburg's most prominent citizen was **Carl Sandburg,** noted poet, socialist, biographer, historian, minstrel and lover of humanity. Sandburg lived in Galesburg until he was 24 years old. His birthplace, 331 E. Third St., the second house east of the Chicago, Burlington and Quincy Railroad tracks, is now a museum. The house is a three-room cottage bought by August Sandburg, Carl's father, in the fall of 1873. Recently a room has been added to the rear of the cottage to house Sandburg exhibits and memorabilia.

Carl Sandburg Park is located behind the birthplace. Legend says that Sandburg was so taken with the spot's beauty that he requested it to be his final resting place.

In 1966, a memorial named **Remembrance Rock,** after Sandburg's only novel, was erected here. The memorial is a large, red granite boulder unearthed during highway construction northeast of Galesburg. It is a glacial remnant and product of the prairie.

Sandburg's ashes were placed beneath Remembrance Rock in 1967. Ten years later his wife, Lilian Paula Sandburg, was buried beside him.

The house is located in the southwest section of Galesburg. Enter Galesburg via the Main Street exit off I-74 and follow directional signs through the town. For more information or group appointments, call (309) 342-2361. Museum hours are Tuesday through Saturday 9–noon, 1–5 p.m., Sunday 1–5 p.m.; closed on all state holidays.

The **Galesburg Railroad Museum** is at South Seminary and Mulberry streets. The museum houses a Pullman parlor car, locomotive #3006 and caboose #13501 among other railroad memorabilia. The museum was once the Burlington-Northern Depot. Tours of the trains are available during **Old Railroad Days** held the second weekend of June. Regular hours are Wednesday, Saturday and Sunday noon–4 p.m.; (309) 343-3421 or 343-6622.

Galesburg holds an annual national **Stearman Fly-In,** generally in the fall. Stearmans are the biplane trainers that gave wings to more military pilots than any other aircraft series in the world. The celebration lasts five days with a cocktail party, slide show featuring past fly-ins, commercial exhibits, mini-air show, Stearman contests, aerobatic competition, short-field takeoff, flour-bombing, spot landing and formation flying contests. For information call the Galesburg Chamber of Commerce, (309) 343-6409.

Railroad Days are also a yearly event in Galesburg. Railroad memorabilia, a street fair, a carnival, antiques, bike races, hot air balloons and gandy olympics—a spike driving competition by Burlington Northern and Santa Fe employees—are part of the festivities. There are also tours of Galesburg's historic sites, firefighters' water fights and bicycle tours. Railroad Days are usually in early June. For exact dates write the Galesburg Chamber of Commerce, 154 E. Simmons St., Galesburg, IL 61401, or call (309) 343-1194.

Knox College, Cherry and South streets, (309) 343-0112, was built in 1857 and has been described as "a monument to the vision of the founding fathers of both the college and city." Old Main, the administration building, was restored and stabilized during the 1930s. It is registered as a national landmark and is an example of American Gothic Revival architecture. Old Main is the only building left standing where Lincoln and Douglas debated. Hours are 8 a.m.–4 p.m.

Knox County Scenic Drive along the Mississippi River is a self-guided tour. The first two weeks in October are a festival with music, flea markets, arts and crafts exhibits and a mock Civil War battle. For information and a map call Galesburg Chamber of Commerce, (309) 343-6409.

Mason County

Some of the greatest concentrations of wild ducks and geese in the nation are to be found in the **Chautauqua National Wildlife Refuge** in Mason County. These feathered creatures contribute to the area's reputation as a hunting and fishing paradise.

The Chautauqua National Wildlife Refuge is a vital link in the chain of resting, feeding and wintering areas for migratory birds along the Mississippi Flyway. During the annual migration, ducks and geese are often so numerous their masses darken the sun.

The refuge has 4,500 acres of land and water where wild ducks and geese can be observed each fall and winter. The average peak concentration during early winter exceeds 100,000 ducks and up to 40,000 Canada, blue and snow geese. Mallards make up most of the duck population, with smaller numbers of wood ducks, pintail, widgeon, black duck, blue-winged teal, scaup, shoveler, gadwall, goldeneye and mergansers.

The wood duck is the most common nester in the refuge. They normally rest in natural cavities in hardwood timber, but they have adapted to nesting boxes erected on the refuge.

Bald eagles winter in several concentrated groups here. More than 240 eagles have been counted along the river. Eagles usually arrive in October and stay until the ice disappears in the spring.

More than 275 species of birds reside on the refuge. Great blue herons, green herons, great egrets and black-crowned night herons are generally summer residents. Marsh, water and shorebirds are common during the spring and fall, and their migration is spectacular during August and early September.

The refuge is open to the public and an interpretive foot trail is located in the headquarters site. Roads adjacent to portions of the refuge provide opportunities for viewing wildlife without disturbing them.

Fishing, mushroom and berry picking and hiking are permitted. Lake Chautauqua is known for its bluegill, crappie and catfish fishing especially during April, May and early June.

Waterfowl hunting is permitted in the Liverpool section, located outside Lake Chautauqua.

For additional information contact the Refuge Manager, Chautauqua National Wildlife Refuge, R.R. 2, Havana, IL 62644; (309) 535-2290. The refuge is eight miles northeast of Havana on the Manito blacktop. A sign marks the entrance.

The **Jack Wolf Memorial Fish Hatchery,** four miles west of Manito on Oil Well Road, has 160 acres within the Sand Ridge State Forest. The hatchery is named after the late Jacob John "Jake" Wolf, who was once Deputy Director of the Department of Conservation for the State of Illinois. Wolf is remembered as a friend of the outdoor sportsman. During his career as a state legislator and as a member of the Department of Conservation, numerous conservation bills were passed that benefited sportsmen statewide.

The complex includes a 36,000-square-foot hatchery building, 56 indoor rearing tanks, spawning and egg incubation facilities, modern fish harvest, and distribution and feeding systems. Outside are 22 acres of solar ponds that use energy from the sun to heat water for fish production, 28 rearing raceways and seven brood raceways.

Specialties of the hatchery are chinook, coho salmon, rainbow and brown trout, walleye, muskellunge, northern pike, striped bass, bluegill, channel catfish and large- and smallmouth bass. The fish produced at the hatchery are used to stock Lake Michigan, private farm ponds, state-owned lakes, reservoirs, and streams and rivers. Anticipated production at the hatchery is 42 million fish annually.

Tours are on a self-guided basis, although employee-guided tours can be scheduled for large groups. Visiting hours are 8:30 a.m.–3:30 p.m. daily; (309) 968-7531.

McDonough County

Founded in 1899, **Western Illinois University,** 900 W. Adams, is an important landmark in Macomb and throughout the western part of the state; (309) 295-1414. Over 12,000 students attend the institution.

On campus is the Western Museum, on the third floor of Sherman Hall. Its collections feature Civil War memorabilia, American Indian costumes, antique farm implements and historical materials from the region. Open Monday through Friday 9 a.m.–4 p.m. during the school year; 1 p.m.–4 p.m. during the summer session; (309) 298-1727. Free.

The university library is known for its unusual pinwheel floor design and a six-story atrium with exhibits and displays throughout. Housing more than 60,000 volumes, it ranks among the top ten largest libraries in the country for nondoctoral degree-granting universities.

On the square in downtown Macomb, the stately old brick **courthouse** is worth a visit, too. Built in the summer of 1872 at a cost of $155,370, the recently renovated building still serves as the center of government. For that matter, there's plenty of history in Macomb. To begin with, the city, founded in 1830, is itself named after Gen. Alexander Macomb, a hero of the War of 1812.

The **Clarence Waston/Wiley Schoolhouse Museum,** 301 W. Calhoun, is a restored 1877 one-room schoolhouse, evocative of the days of pigtails and inkwells. Open 8:30–noon and 1–4:30 p.m. Monday through Friday. Pick up brochures on other things to see and do in the area here, as well, as the museum also serves as the Macomb Chamber of Commerce Tourist Information Center; (309) 837-4855.

Home of the McDonough County Preservation Society is

the **Old Bailey House,** an 1887 Eastlake-style residence at 100 S. Campbell, built by the founder of Macomb's Union National Bank.

The nation's leading manufacturer of art pottery and floral containers is based in Macomb. **Haeger Potteries,** 411 W. Calhoun, has free 30-minute guided plant tours daily, Monday through Friday at 8:45 and 10:45 a.m., 1:15 and 1:45 p.m. The showroom, where you can buy some of their lovely creations, is open Monday through Saturday 8:30 a.m.–5 p.m. and Sunday 10 a.m.–5 p.m.; (309) 833-2171.

Theatergoers have several options: The **Pat Crane Memorial Playhouse** is a popular community theater, with in-the-round productions running from September through May. Call (309) 837-1828 for ticket information. The playhouse is on St. Francis Road, two miles south of Macomb. Western Illinois University has its own **Summer Music Theater** at Brown Hall; (309) 298-1254. And the **Argyle Summer Theater** presents free historical dramas each Saturday night in July at **Argyle Lake State Park;** (309) 298-1543.

The park, seven miles west of Macomb and two miles north of Colchester off U.S. 136, has 1,148 acres of recreational land within its boundaries, including the 95-acre Argyle Lake. Interestingly, the State Department of Conservation in 1970 showed a remarkable sense of doing a job right when, after 20 years of bad fishing, they simply drained the whole lake, removed undesirable species and restocked the lake with the fish they wanted. The park takes its name from a group of early settlers of Scottish descent, who called the area Argyle Hollow. Through here passed the old Galena-to-Beardstown stagecoach in the early 1800s. Today, the park offers visitors picnicking, boating and fishing (for bluegill, largemouth bass, crappie and channel catfish), camping (electrical outlets available), hiking, and a summer interpretive program. Boats and canoes can be rented. The park is open year-round and winter brings cross-country skiing, snowmobiling trails, ice skating, and sledding. For more information, contact the Site Superintendent, R.R. 2, Colchester, IL 62326; (309) 776-3422.

Menard County

If the Midwest were Arabia, then surely **New Salem Village** would be its Mecca, for thousands of pilgrims journey here each year for a glimpse of the relics of Lincoln. The state park, two miles south of the county seat, Petersburg, on SR 97, is a reconstruction of the village in which Lincoln lived from 1831–37.

Here, homes, shops and taverns take you back to the time when Lincoln was just beginning his political career. He served here as postmaster and deputy surveyor and was defeated for election to the Illinois General Assembly in 1832, then elected two years later.

The 1835 **Onstot Cooper Shop** is the only original building on the site, and it was there that Lincoln studied law books late in the night. The **Lincoln-Berry** store is an authentic recreation of the general store in which Lincoln was a partner. At the **Rutledge Tavern** lived his first love, Ann Rutledge (who is buried in Oakwood Cemetery in Petersburg).

Costumed interpreters man the shops and exhibits, so you may encounter a blacksmith at his forge, a baker taking freshly baked bread from the oven, or a candlemaker at his craft. Oxen and other farm animals are part of the scene. Inside the park, flowers and plants have been planted for historic authenticity. Vegetable gardens and herb gardens are tucked behind the cabins and wild plum, blackberry, gooseberry, and other trees and shrubs add to the look of the 1830s village.

At the **Kelso Hollow Amphitheater,** which is part of the park, nightly performances of the legend of Lincoln are presented by the Great American People Show. Mid-June through mid-August, closed Mondays; (217) 632-7755.

The park has camping facilities available on the grounds (178 campsites, showers and electric hookups available). Admission to the park is free. For more information, contact Site Superintendent, R.R. 1, Box 244A, Petersburg, IL 62675; (217) 632-7953.

Take a ride on the paddlewheel steamboat *Talisman*, a replica of the only steamboat to successfully navigate the Sangamon River. Forty-five-minute trips begin at the dock just steps away from New Salem Village. The 2½-mile excursion operates daily from May to Labor Day and then on weekends only through October; (217) 632-2219.

In Petersburg, at Jackson and Eighth streets, is the **Edgar Lee Masters Memorial Home**. The poet and author of *Spoon River Anthology* lived here as a boy. Much of his work reflects the feeling of this part of Illinois. Restored to its 1875 period, the home holds memorabilia of the family and his work. Open Memorial Day through Labor Day daily except Monday. Admission free; (217) 632-7363. Masters is also buried in the town's Oakwood Cemetery.

Peoria

Peoria is one of Illinois's larger cities and offers attractions for both the nature- and cultural-minded tourist.

The **Glen Oak Park Botanical Garden,** 2218 N. Prospect Rd., Peoria, IL 61603-4321, (309) 685-4321, has a rose garden with more than 800 all-American award-winning selections. The All-Seasons Garden has plants selected for their unique characteristics that provide beauty all year-round. The herb garden has plants that are pleasant to smell and add zest to culinary arts.

The Conservatory is the permanent home of a collection of tropical plants and fragile specimens and the Bio-Center has education programs, workshops, films and seminars.

Admission to the gardens is free, and they are open from dawn to dusk. The Conservatory is open from 8 a.m.–4 p.m.

The **Lakeview Museum of Arts and Sciences,** 1125 W. Lake Ave., Peoria, IL 61614, (309) 686-7000, has antiques, archeology, astronomy, geology, folk art, music, wildlife and movie exhibitions. The main exhibit is Man and Nature: The Changing Relationship. It is a multimedia program telling the story of mankind's ties with nature from prehistoric to present times.

The Decorative Art Gallery has English, French and American furniture from the eighteenth to the twentieth centuries. Other collections include fine arts, anthropology, history and natural sciences.

The Planetarium gives laser light concerts and has a museum shop, sales/rental gallery and bookstore.

Museum hours are Tuesday through Saturday 10 a.m.–4 p.m., Wednesday evening 7–9 p.m. and Sunday noon–5 p.m. The museum is closed on Mondays and major holidays. Admission to the museum is free; the Planetarium show is $2 for adults, $1 for children and seniors.

The **Wildlife Prairie Park** began as the project of the Forest Park Foundation. The theme was native North American animals living in natural habitat enclosures with other areas of the park portraying Illinois's natural history. A 24-inch gauge railroad system travels through the park.

From May through October, hours are 10 a.m.–6:30 p.m.

except Thursdays, when the park is open until 8:30 p.m. The first three weekends in November, hours are 9 a.m.–4:30 p.m., Saturday and Sunday only. From December through April, the park is open on Sunday only, 9:30 a.m.–3 p.m. A gift shop and country store are on the grounds.

The park offers special events that include the Illinois Art League show, tree-planting parties and Pops on the Prairie Concerts with the Peoria Symphony Orchestra.

The park is located ten miles west of downtown Peoria, off I-74 via exit 82 on Taylor Road. Admission is $3 for adults, $1.50 for teens and $1 for children; (309) 676-0998.

The **Peoria Historical Society,** 942 N.E. Glen Oak, (309) 674-1921, offers scenic and historic bus tours of Peoria. The tour starts downtown, travels through the Fort Clark site on the Illinois riverbank, through the historic courthouse plaza and city hall. Narrated group tours are available for half a day or a full day and include lunch. For information contact the society.

Two houses that are of interest and available for viewing are the **Flanagan House,** 942 N.E. Glen Oak Ave., and the **Pettengill-Morron House,** 1212 W. Moss Ave. Both houses were constructed in the 1800s and are furnished in period style. Call (309) 674-1921 for tours. Admission is $2 for adults, 50 cents for children under 12. The houses are open Sunday 2–4:30 p.m. March through December, or by appointment.

The *Julia Belle Swain* is the last steamer on the Illinois River and one of the five river steamboats remaining in the United States. The steamboat offers excursions from the foot of Main Street in Peoria. Sightseeing trips of 1½ hours are Friday, Saturday and Sunday at 1, 3 and 5 p.m.; $5 for adults, $2 for children under 13.

Moonlight dance trips on Saturday nights at 7:30 p.m. and 10 p.m. are $6 per person.

Two-day river cruises to Starved Rock State Park and back every Monday and Wednesday during June, July and August are $150 per person and include meals, entertainment and lodging. Call (309) 674-5820 for more information.

Bacon's Farm, 3300 Willow Knolls Rd., was a model of contemporary dairy husbandry and a prosperous dairy, but after the death of Dr. Bacon in 1940, the farm fell into disrepair. The complex is being restored as a regional attraction with a restaurant, live theater and specialty shops, such as the Back Porch gift shop and O'Leary's restaurant.

The **Cabaret Music Theater** is Peoria's only full-time professional theater company. For box office information call (309) 692-9500 between 1–9 p.m. daily.

Pike County

Pittsfield, the county seat of Pike County, was a genuine transplant of New England culture when it was founded in 1833. The settlers came from Pittsfield, Massachusetts, and purchased the site from the federal government for $200.

Pork-packing became the chief local industry and Pittsfield now has the distinction of being the "Pork Capital of the World," with 400,000 to 500,000 hogs marketed there annually. Pittsfield and Pike County residents celebrate **Pig Days** with a day of activities and pork sandwiches and a pork chop dinner. The festival is held during the summer and the Chamber of Commerce is happy to supply information. Contact them at P.O. Box 283, Pittsfield, IL 62363, or call (217) 285-2971.

Pittsfield also has a **Fall Festival** in September that signals the beginning of the harvest season. Again, the Chamber of Commerce has information.

Sights to see in Pittsfield are the home of **John Nicolay,** President Lincoln's private secretary. The home is now owned by a private citizen but can be viewed from the street. Nicolay collaborated with John Hay, a personal friend of Lincoln's, in writing a biography of the president. The house is at 500 W. Washington St.

The home of town philanthropist **William Ross** no longer stands, but a marker designates the site near the city limits. Ross's mansion was destroyed by fire in 1896. Abraham Lincoln was an overnight guest here when he debated with Stephen A. Douglas in Pittsfield in 1858.

The **Lewis M. Grigsby, Sr., home,** 830 E. Washington St., was built by Colonel Ross's daughter, Mrs. Earl Grigsby, and her friend Mrs. F. M. Lewis, Sr., in 1930. Six generations of the Ross family have resided in Pittsfield, and four generations have lived in this house.

The Pike County Historical Society has been restoring the **East School Building,** listed in the *National Register of Historic Places.* The building, built in 1866, is now a museum and John Wood Community College Learning Center. The pride of the society is the renovated clock in the tower. The building was designed by John M. Van Osdel, the "grandfather of Illinois architecture," and is one of the two remaining examples of his work.

The local community theater group, the **Pittsfield Theatre Guild,** presents five productions a year and is based in the school building. The Chamber of Commerce has information.

The **Pike County Courthouse** is a unique landmark in the town square. Built in 1893–94, it is octagonal in shape and made of Berea stone. The building was designed by Henry Elliot of Chicago and is listed by the Illinois Arts Council as one of Illinois's ten most outstanding examples of courthouse architecture.

Griggsville is the "Purple Martin Capital of the World." For those who are wondering, purple martins are birds, the largest of the swallows, which feed only on flying insects, thus cleaning the air of millions of insects every day.

Purple Martin Junction is a ten-acre complex on SR 107 at the south end of Griggsville. A factory that makes aluminum martin houses and an experimental martin colony are on the grounds. The best time to view the martins at this colony is from May to July. For information call (217) 833-2393.

Pike County has its share of natural beauty. Bound by the Mississippi River on the west and the Illinois River on the east, it has rolling countryside and majestic bluffs. Streams, ponds and small lakes abound for fishing, boating and swimming. Hunting and camping is also plentiful.

Pine Lakes Camping and Fishing Resort, 1½ mile north of U.S. 36 near Pittsfield, has camping facilities that include water and electric hookups, laundromat, camp store, recreation room, paddleboat rental, rowboats, bathhouse and snack bar. Enjoy swimming with attendants on duty, fishing in a 45-acre lake, horseshoe pits, hayrides and playground.

Besides campgrounds, six two-bedroom cottages are available for rent. Contact Pine Lakes Resort, R.R. 3, Box 130A, Pittsfield, IL 62363; (217) 285-6719.

Schuyler County

Now a trading center for coal mining and a grain and fruit growing region, Rushville began as a tiny wilderness village of 12 families in 1825. It was named for a famous Philadelphia surgeon, Dr. Benjamin Rush. It has stayed a small town with only 3,348 residents.

The community is rich in nineteenth-century history. During the Black Hawk War, Abraham Lincoln and his troops camped near Rushville. In 1844, it is believed that Governor Ford left Springfield with a company of militia and camped overnight in the town square. A tablet in the center of the town square reads, "Abraham Lincoln addressed the people of Rushville on October 20th, 1858." Lincoln also practiced law in the county courthouse that once stood on this spot.

When Stephen A. Douglas came to Rushville to speak in the senatorial campaign of 1858, his followers arranged a welcome that would be remembered in the town's history. They borrowed a cannon from the nearby community of Beardston, brought it over to the town square, and loaded it with a heavy charge of powder and wet scraps of leather. When the salute to Douglas was fired, the cannon was blown into pieces, miraculously hurting no one.

The **Schuyler County Courthouse** dates back from 1881. It is a two-story building of faded brick and topped with a square clock tower. The cornerstone is dated according to the Masonic calendar and reads June 24 A.L. 5881. The first county building was a log cabin on the north side of the square. In 1829 it was replaced by a plain unornamented brick building, which served until the present courthouse was built on the corner of Lafayette and Congress streets.

The **Schuyler-Brown County Historical Society** at 200 S. Congress (on U.S. 24, just one block from the courthouse corner) displays geneological materials and the history of Schuyler and Brown counties. The center of the building is an old jailhouse. A collection of undertakers' sticks, used to measure the deceased for custom-built coffins, is on display. The society's museum is open daily 1–5 p.m., March through November and on Sundays the rest of the year.

At the same location is the **Jail Museum,** open Friday, Saturday and Sunday 1–5 p.m., April 1 to November 1. Special exhibits change monthly. The museum is open at other times by appointment only. Call (217) 322-6975 for more information about these museums.

Scripps Park was formerly the 80-acre farm of Edward Wyllis Scripps, founder of the Scripps-Howard newspaper chain. The park was given to the town in 1922 by Scripps and his two sisters, Virginia and Ellen Browning Scripps. The latter contributed the $100,000 Community House that marks the site of the Scripps homestead, the birthplace of Edward Wyllis Scripps. The park is located outside of Rushville, southwest of the junction of U.S. 67 and U.S. 24; (217) 322-3028.

Warren County

For fans of old TV westerns, the most important sightseeing stop in the county is surely the house in Monmouth in which **Wyatt Earp** was born on March 19, 1848; 913 S. Sixth St. (now a private residence). A memorial to Earp stands in Monmouth Park. While he found a final resting place in California, many of his relatives are buried in Monmouth's **Pioneer Cemetery** on East Archer near Fifth Street. In fact, a walk around the old cemetery gives you some historical perspective on the town, which was founded in 1831.

A county landmark is **Monmouth College,** established in 1853 by a group of Scottish Presbyterians who pioneered the settlement of this part of the state. The campus has many attractive brick buildings in the Greek Revival style. The white-framed **Holt House,** at 402 E. First Ave., is the birthplace of Pi Beta Phi Sorority. Architecture buffs will enjoy a drive down East Broadway, as well, where the homes are memories of a more gracious period. Historic district status for the area is being pursued.

In front of the castle-like 1895 Richardsonian Romanesque county courthouse in Monmouth stands a statue of Gen. Abner C. Harding, a hero at the second battle of Fort Donaldson during the Civil War.

And while Dixon claims the title as Ronald Reagan's boyhood home, Monmouth, too, shares the honor, for the family lived here briefly during the president's early years, at 218 S. Seventh St. (now a private residence).

DeNovo Ceramics, historically known as Western Stoneware Company, 521 Sixth Ave., (309) 734-2161, is the oldest maker of pottery and stoneware in the Midwest. The maple leaf emblem that appeared on Western Stoneware's jugs and crocks produced here came from Monmouth's epithet as Maple City (especially well-earned in the fall when the city's thousands of maple trees are ablaze with color). Though no factory tours are available, their retail outlet, **The Pottery Barn,** located at U.S.

34 and U.S. 67, is open daily. Hours are 8:30 a.m.–4:30 p.m. except Sunday, noon–4:30 p.m.

Each year in early September, the Warren County **Prime Beef Festival** is held in Monmouth. There are livestock shows, parades, a rodeo and carnival. Call (309) 734-3181 for more information.

For recreation during the warmer months, the 18 holes of **Gibson Woods Golf Course** are open to the public. The course is adjacent to Monmouth Park on U.S. 34 immediately northeast of Monmouth, (309) 734-9968.

Monmouth Airport, northeast of town on U.S. 34, is the oldest continually operating airport in the state.

Out in the rural part of the county, visit the **County Historical Museum** at Roseville.

Off the Beaten Path in Southeastern Illinois

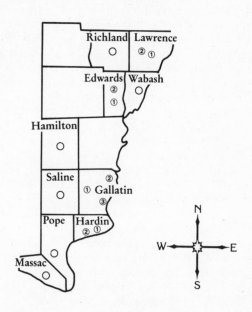

SOUTHEAST

Edwards
1. Albion
2. Bone Gap

Gallatin
1. Equality
2. New Haven
3. Shawneetown

Hamilton
O McLeansboro

Hardin
1. Cave-in-Rock
2. Rosiclare

Lawrence
1. Lawrenceville
2. Sumner

Massac
O Metropolis

Pope
O Brownfield

Richland
O Olney

Saline
O Harrisburg

Wabash
O Mt. Carmel

Edwards County

Edwards County is known as the **Chowder Capital of the World.** The aroma of this fragrant dish can be detected around the county any time from June through September.

There is no exact information on when chowder became popular here, but records from the time of the Civil War indicate that it was enjoyed as early as the 1860s.

Chowder is generally cooked in large black kettle cauldrons, ranging in size from 20 to 70 gallons. A variety of ingredients are added to boiling water, among them tomatoes because chowder time traditionally starts when the tomatoes ripen and closes with the heavy frost.

Several communities in Edwards County hold chowders, and the Edwards County Historical Society, 212 W. Main St., Albion, IL 62806, (618) 445-2631, has information on Albion and other community's chowders.

The **Albion Pagoda** in Albion was erected in 1914 and is the town's pride. The first pagoda was built around the mineral water well in 1890. The waters were said to cure rheumatism, kidney and urinary troubles, "derangements of the stomach and bowels," and many other afflictions. When the original pagoda deteriorated, a second one was built in the same location; then in 1906 the current two-story structure replaced the two previous ones. The third pagoda was designed by architect W. E. Felix of Fairfield and constructed as a community program by the Albion Women's Beautifying Club.

The pagoda is octagonal with eight brick columns. The roof is made of red clay, resembling the roofs of the pagodas in the Far East.

Bone Gap is a name that brings images of hunting and Indians to mind. The **Indian Hill Museum** in Bone Gap has exhibits of pioneer life, woodworking and blacksmith shops from early railroad days.

Besides a collection of Indian artifacts, which includes a totem pole made locally around 1900, the museum has family heirlooms and historical items pertaining to the English settlements in the Wabash Valley.

Museum founders Norman and Sandy Reid's main objective is to educate the younger generation and create an air of reminiscence for others. Here you'll find a 1920 Keck-Gonnerman steam engine, which was used to power a sawmill and threshing machine, more than 10,000 Indian artifacts, including some dating back to the Archaic period 10,000 years ago, and a Regina music box with a cherry wood case and hand-painted view of the Midwest that dates to 1861.

Norman Reid also has a collection of more than 300 guns, which includes handguns ranging from the Civil War period to the 1880 period, and an ancient buffalo skull that was found on the plains more than 107 years ago.

The museum is open May 1 through October 31 every day except Monday from 10 a.m.–6 p.m. and November 1 through April 30 every day except Monday and Thursday from 9 a.m.–4 p.m.; (618) 446-3277. The museum is on Route 3 in Bone Gap (from Albion take SR 130 to Route 3).

Gallatin County

While today, we can get in our cars and speed hundreds of miles over broad, smoothly paved interstate highways, travelers in the first part of the nineteenth century turned to rivers and riverboats for efficient travel. And of those rivers, the Ohio was one of the longest and most frequently chosen routes, an interstate expressway from Pennsylvania all the way to the Mississippi River. Thus, the importance of Gallatin County and its seat, Shawneetown, are clearly understood in terms of a river port. Today, one of the world's longest span cantilever bridges crosses the Ohio at Shawneetown.

Shawnee Indians had a village here in the mid-1700s and burial mounds can be seen throughout the area. The earliest white settlers arrived around 1800. In 1810, the federal government laid out Shawneetown on the river, and it quickly became a major port and gateway for immigrants into the new frontier. In 1814, it became the first incorporated town in Illinois. A ferry service, crossing the river into Kentucky, was begun. Four years later, the U.S. Land Office for southeastern Illinois opened at Shawneetown. Adding to the economic growth of the community were the nearby saltworks at Equality, which supplied an important pioneer commodity and shipped salt throughout the region. Thus, Shawneetown became an important financial center in the American westward movement.

The first bank in the territory opened here in 1816. Known as the **John Marshall Bank** for the early merchant who began it in his house, the brick structure has been reconstructed by the local historical society and is open for tours by appointment.

A second bank, the 1839 **Shawneetown Bank,** is a handsome Greek Revival building with Doric columns supporting a portico. (It's now listed in the *National Register of Historic Places.*) For its construction, sandstone was floated down the Ohio by flatboat from quarries in the East. A favorite local story is of the time when businessmen from the tiny village of Chicago rode to Shawneetown to ask bankers there for a loan. They were refused on the grounds that Chicago was much too far from Shawneetown to ever prosper. For more information about both of these banks, call the Southeastern Illinois Planning Commission at (618) 252-7463.

The Ohio River proved a blessing and a curse for the community. Major floods periodically struck the town—in 1884, 1898, 1913 and in 1937. In 1937, residents rebuilt their community in the hills three miles inland. In Old Shawneetown, the original settlement, many of the old landmarks are part of Shawneetown State Memorial Park, on the banks of the river.

The most famous visitor of all to visit Shawneetown was Marquis de LaFayette. The Revolutionary War hero was honored here at a reception at the Rawlings' Hotel on May 7, 1825. Gov. Edward Coles greeted the soldier at the waterfront. The hotel burned in 1904.

Equality, at the west side of the county near SR 142 and SR 13, was the site of the United States Salines, salty springs first discovered by the Indians. Later, French and American settlers made salt at the site. As an important early industry, the springs became the property of first the federal, then the state government. Andrew Jackson, before becoming president, attempted to lease these springs. Today only some crumbling foundations remain. A mural in the Gallatin County Courthouse depicts these salt-making operations.

Three miles east of Equality, off SR 1 south of the junction of SR 1 and SR 13, is the **Old Slave House,** the county's top visitor attraction. This mansion, named Hickory Hill, was erected in 1834 by John Crenshaw, one of the lessees of the government salt springs, who became quite wealthy in that trade. Another trade in which it is suggested he made money was the slave trade, and the third floor of the house holds cells with anchor chains on the floors. Open April through November, daily 9 a.m.–6 p.m.

At the northwest border of the county, at New Haven, once

stood the mill of Jonathan Boone, brother of Daniel Boone. Jonathan Boone died here in 1808. A state historical marker records the spot.

Ridgway, in the center of the county, is the popcorn capital of the state and host to **Popcorn Days** each September. Call the Chamber of Commerce at (618) 272-7500 for more information. Blevins Popcorn Factory is located here.

Two miles off SR 1 and 11 miles north of Cave-in-Rock is **Pounds Hollow,** an especially scenic recreation area. A 22-acre lake is nestled under steep bluffs. Follow Rim Rock Trail around the lake to the prehistoric Pounds Wall, a 7,000-year-old Indian structure. It is uncertain whether this Pounds Wall, once 8–10 feet high, was used as a fortification or for killing buffalo. Most experts guess the latter use, because a buffalo wallow is nearby. Buffalo would have been rounded up against the wall and slaughtered.

Hamilton County

The prize of McLeansboro, the county seat, is the **McCoy Memorial Library,** on the west side of the public square. The Cloud family built this handsome brick Victorian mansion, with a central tower and unique roof line, in 1884. It is listed in the *National Register of Historic Places.* Along with an 8,000-volume collection, the library boasts countless antiques on display for visitors. A central feature of the home is the number of noteworthy fireplaces throughout the structure. On the second floor, the **Hamilton County Historical Society Museum** exhibits souvenirs of the area's past. Open Wednesday and Friday 1–4 p.m. Admission $1, children under 12 free. The library is open every day but Sunday.

Next to the library building and once a residence is the **People's National Bank,** built by the same family, the Clouds, and also listed in the *National Register.*

For a bite of something to eat, the hearty fare at **Pat's City and Country Cafe** on SR 14 East is some of the best in the county. Stop for shopping at the **Southfork Antique Mall,** 105 E. Broadway in McLeansboro.

Hardin County

At the southeastern tip of Illinois, on the Ohio River, Hardin County has long been a stopping place for restless pioneers moving west. One of the first was Samuel Mason, an officer of the Continental Army and renegade son of an important Virginia family, who came to Illinois territory in 1797. Discovering a deep cavern on the bluff overlooking the river, Mason set himself up in business, advertising over the arched cavern opening, "Liquor Vault and House of Entertainment." His business, though, was not innkeeping, but rather piracy, and he handily plundered gullible travelers and flatboat crews. When his notoriety caught up with him, he fled, leaving the cave to a long line of fellow thieves.

Today, **Cave-in-Rock** is part of a state park of the same name, with facilities for picnicking, hiking, boating, fishing and camping (60 sites, 35 with electric hookups). Off SR 1 and open year-round, Box 338, Cave-in-Rock, IL 62919; (618) 289-4325.

From the little town here runs the only ferry on the Ohio River that shuttles cars and passengers. It operates 6 a.m.–6 p.m. daily. The third weekend in July each year, Cave-in-Rock holds **Frontier Days** to commemorate its historic past. The event features a parade, beauty pageant, carnival, square dancing and craft exhibits.

Four miles north of Rosiclare near the junction of SR 34 and SR 146 is the **Old Illinois Iron Furnace,** the first in Illinois. It began in 1837 on colorfully named Hog Thief Creek, eventually supporting 100 families. Some of its production was used at the Mound City Naval Shipyards to clad gunboats during the Civil War. The furnace was abandoned in 1883. There are two interpretive trails at the site along with an inviting "swimming hole" in Big Creek.

At Rosiclare is the **Mineral Museum,** depicting the area's mining past with samples of minerals, tools and pictoral exhibits. The museum was founded by the Rosiclare Lead and Fluorspar Mining Company, once the world's largest fluorspar operation. On Walnut Street; open year-round, 9 a.m.–5 p.m. Monday through Friday. For weekend tours, call Millard Mick at (618) 285-3483.

At Elizabethtown is the **Old Rose Hotel,** on SR 146 at the Ohio River. Dating from 1813, it's the oldest hotel building in the state. The hotel was operational until 1972, the longest run

Old Illinois Iron Furnace

of any hotel in Illinois. For an appointment for a guided tour, call (618) 287-2491 Monday through Friday.

Seven miles west from Cave-in-Rock and about four miles south of SR 146 is **Tower Rock Park Recreation Area,** where the scenery is a fine example of that found throughout the Shawnee National Forest, which covers the county. The Ohio River runs along the southern edge of the park, providing opportunities for fishing and boating. Camping and picnicking are available at Tower Rock, as well. Ranger's Office: (618) 287-2201.

Lawrence County

One mile northeast of Sumner in Lawrence County is **Red Hills State Park**, a 948-acre park of high wooded hills, deep ravines, meadows and year-round springs. Hickory, oak, sycamore, maple, gum, crab, walnut and apple trees grow in abundance in this area. Squirrels, doves, woodcocks, quail and rabbit live and multiply in this haven for nature lovers and sportsmen.

U.S. 50 divides the park into two sections and the park itself is a historical crossroad, the westernmost edge being the first land in Illinois ceded by the Indians to the United States government. The border line runs through the park from southwest to northeast and was set by a treaty made in 1795 at Greenville, Ohio, by Gen. Anthony Wayne and the Indians. The Indians relinquished all claims to the land northwest of the Ohio River and east of a specified line. The area was called the Vincennes Tract.

The name Red Hill comes from the peak by the same name, which is the highest point along the Baltimore and Oriole Railroad between Cincinnati and St. Louis. Red Hill is topped by a tower and a cross, constructed and financed by residents cooperating in an interdenominational council.

The park has picnicking, fishing, boating, camping and hunting facilities. A park interpreter conducts summer recreation programs. There is a trail through the woods and other areas suitable for hiking. Ice fishing and ice skating are permitted in season. For more details contact: Red Hills State Park, R.R. 4, Sumner, IL 62466; (618) 936-2469.

Lawrence County residents like to celebrate and in fall there are four festivals: **Sumner Fall Festival,** the first weekend after Labor Day; **St. Francisville Chestnut Festival**, the first weekend in October; the **Lawrenceville Fall Festival;** and **Bridgeport Oil Days.** For exact dates and a list of activities, contact the Lawrence County Chamber of Commerce, 1104 Jefferson St., Lawrenceville, IL 62349; (618) 943-3516.

Massac County

The people of Metropolis will swear to you that Superman really exists. Metropolis claims to be the hometown of the fictional movie and cartoon character Superman. A billboard of Superman welcoming visitors to Metropolis greets you as you enter the town, and another portrait of their hero adorns the water tower. The Chamber of Commerce boasts the only official Superman phone booth, where you can actually speak with the Man of Steel. And just for the sake of continuity, the local newspaper is called the *Daily Planet.*

An annual **Superman Celebration** usually falls on the second weekend in June, runs for two days, and includes a beauty pageant, style show, arts and crafts show, street dance, flea market and Superman Run.

Metropolis is also the home of the **Massac Historic Museum,** Fourth and Market streets. This two-story brick house was restored to its original design and is open on Sunday from 2–4 p.m. Call (618) 524-5120 for more information.

Massac County has a historical legend stemming from **Fort Massac.** One of five former French forts in the Illinois park system, it borders the Ohio River at the southern tip of the state.

Indians were believed to have first used the site because of its strategic location on the river. In the early 1540s, Spanish explorer Hernando de Soto and his soldiers constructed a fortification here for protection from hostile Indians.

Legend tells us that during the first half of the eighteenth century, many soldiers were massacred here by Indians, thus the name Fort Massacre, later shortened to Massac.

Reconstruction of the fort and an accompanying museum began in the fall of 1971 and was completed in the summer of 1973. Three of the buildings were originally used as living quarters for enlisted men and as means of defense with loopholes for muskets.

The **Fort Massac Museum** houses a miniature replica of the fort, artifacts and a history of the fort. It is open year-round on Wednesday through Sunday 10 a.m.–4:30 p.m. Guided tours are available by appointment. Call (618) 524-9321 for an appointment.

Fort Massac State Park is open daily. The replica of the fort is open 6 a.m.–10 p.m. daily. The park offers picnicking, fishing, boating and camping facilities and two self-guided trails for hiking. Hunting is allowed in season.

For information contact the Site Superintendent, Box 708, Metropolis, IL 62960; (618) 542-4712.

The **Fort Massac Encampment** is an annual festival recreating the atmophere of a military encampment in the Illinois country in the 1700s. Contact the park office for dates and times.

Fort Massac State Park is located 2½ miles west of Metropolis off I-24 on SR 45. The museum and encampment are on the grounds.

Pope County

Kitch-mus-ke-nee-be, or the Great Medicine Waters, was once the Indian name for the area known as **Dixon Springs State Park.** Part of the Illinois Shawnee Hills, the park sits on a giant block of rock, which dropped 200 feet along a fault line that extends northwesterly across Pope County.

The park is about ten miles west of Golconda on SR 146 near the junction of SR 145. This spot was once occupied by the Algonquin Indians who, after the Shawnee tribe had been driven from Tennessee, settled near the mouth of the Wabash River.

The area was named for William Dixon, one of the first white men to build a home here. He obtained a school land warrant in 1848, and his cabin was a landmark for many years. A small community grew up at Dixon Springs, and in the nineteenth century it became a health spa, which attracted hundreds to the seven springs of mineral-enriched water. A bathhouse provided mineral or soft water baths.

The country is hilly and during the rainy season, rivulets cascade down the hills forming waterfalls.

Picnicking, camping, biking and hiking are permitted. Enjoy the self-guided 1.7-mile nature trail or the modern swimming pool supplied by spring water, with lifeguard and bathhouse facilities. A concession stand is located near the pool as well as picnic shelters, playgrounds and drinking water.

The park is open year-round except for holidays. For information contact the Site Superintendent, Dixon Springs State Park, R.R. 1, Brownfield, IL 62911; (618) 949-3394.

Richland County

Olney is the home of the white albino squirrel. Local legend says that the white squirrel first appeared here in 1902. A hunter captured two squirrels, a male and female, and put them on display in a town saloon.

Another townsman heard about the squirrels and sent his son over to get the animals and release them in the woods. As soon as the squirrels were freed, a large fox squirrel jumped down from a tree and killed the male. The son shot the fox squirrel as he tried to attack the female. Weeks later, baby white albino squirrels were seen and the population has increased to about 800 albino squirrels.

A city ordinance has been enacted to protect these special citizens. A white squirrel has the right of way on any street in Olney, and a motorist is fined $25 for running over one. Anyone caught taking one out of the town will also be fined.

Olney residents are also protective of their bird population. At Bird Haven in **Robert Ridgway Memorial Arboretum and Bird Sanctuary,** you can walk and observe nature. Robert Ridgway, a naturalist, scientist, artist and author is famous for his books *Birds of Middle and North America* and *Color Stands and Color Nomenclature.* He was associated with the Smithsonian Institute and was a zoologist for the Survey of the 40th Parallel. He was also an authority in the field of ornithology.

Ridgway purchased the 18 acres of Bird Haven in 1906. By the 1920s the arboretum and bird sanctuary was said to have had the second largest number of plant species, second to a larger tract in Japan.

The Ridgway summer cottage once stood on the grounds, and a replica of the front porch has been reproduced on the cottage site. Dr. Ridgway's grave is on the grounds and is marked by a granite boulder with a bronze plaque with birds sculpted on it.

Bird Haven's hours are from dusk to dawn. For more information, contact Olney City Hall, 300 Whittle Ave., Olney, IL 62450; (618) 395-7302. Bird Haven is a half mile northeast of Olney on East Fork Lake Road.

Olney holds an annual **Arts and Crafts Festival** every fall. It is a performing arts showcase open to amateur and professional fine artists and craftsmen. Contact the Olney Arts Council, P.O. Box 291, Olney, IL 62450, for specific dates and entry information.

Saline County

In the southeast corner of the county, where it joins Gallatin and Hardin counties, the **Garden of the Gods** is one of the state's most dramatic natural attractions. Created more than 200 million years ago from geologic uplifting, spectacular rock outcroppings have been formed through the action of water and wind. The unusual rock formations have been given names by imaginative explorers—Camel Rock, Noah's Ark, Mushroom Rock, Fat Man's Squeeze and Tower of Babel are some of the more colorful ones.

One mile of well-maintained trails and five miles of semideveloped trails allow hikers to trek through the low mountainous region. Part of the **Shawnee National Forest,** which runs across the width of southern Illinois, the Garden of the Gods is a perfect spot for camping. For information on the Garden of the Gods, contact the Shawnee National Forest Headquarters, (618) 253-7114. Just north is the **Saline County Conservation Area** with its **Glen O. Jones Lake.**

Harrisburg, the county seat, was at one time a major center for tobacco growing and, later, coal mining. Here, the **Saline County Area Museum,** 1600 Feazel St., is a popular attraction. Set in a park-like setting are a handful of furnished historic buildings, moved here from around the area. You can visit an 1800s one-room schoolhouse, an old Moravian church, a log cabin, general store, post office and barn. The museum is open every day except Monday 9 a.m.–5 p.m. Admission $1 adults, 50 cents children. On the last Sunday in September, the museum holds an open house, which attracts thousands. For information call (618) 252-4192.

Wabash County

For real nature buffs, **Beall Woods Nature Preserve and State Park,** six miles south of Mount Carmel in Wabash County, is the largest tract of original deciduous forest remaining in the United States and is relatively untouched by man.

There 64 species of trees have been identified, and there is reason to believe that more will be discovered. Approximately 300 trees with trunks greater than 30 inches in circumference at chest height are in the park.

The tract of land that is now the park was under the ownership of the Beall family for more than 102 years. After the death of Laura Beall, the property was sold to a man who intended to clear the land and farm it. Conservation-minded individuals and groups helped to create the original acquisition by the State of Illinois in 1965 by evoking the law of eminent domain against unwilling settlers in order to preserve the virgin woodland for posterity.

Beall Woods is a registered landmark and is listed as the "Forest of the Wabash." The woods are made up of 270 acres of primeval woodland that borders the Wabash River, and the area was dedicated as an Illinois nature preserve to insure that the forest will remain in its natural condition.

Beall Woods is sometimes referred to as the "University of Trees" because it is a living forest community with a natural ecological system containing native plant and animal life. Hikers can view red fox, deer, racoon and pileated woodpeckers, and the forest floor supports a variety of interesting flowers.

There are plenty of hiking trails for those interested. The trails begin at the Red Barn, a remodeled barn that serves as a nature center. It has a display of seeds, native woods of Illinois and Indian arrowheads. Hours are 7 a.m.–4 p.m. daily.

There are also facilities for picnicking and a playground. The park is open year-round except for Christmas and New Year's Day. For information contact the Site Superintendent, Beall Woods Conservation Area, R.R. 2, Mount Carmel, IL 62863; (618) 298-2442. Beall Woods is near Keensburg off SR 1, about six miles south of Mount Carmel.

Off *the Beaten Path*
in Southwestern Illinois

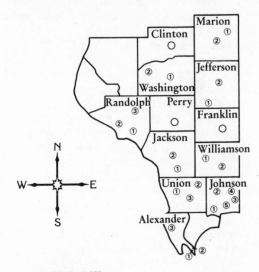

SOUTHWEST

Alexander
1. Cairo
2. Ft. Defiance
3. Thebes

Clinton
O Carlyle

Franklin
O Benton

Jackson
1. Carbondale
2. Murphysboro

Jefferson
1. Benton
2. Mt. Vernon

Johnson
1. Cypress
2. Goreville
3. Robbs
4. Simpson
5. Vienna

Marion
1. Kimundy
2. Salem

Perry
O DuQuoin

Randolph
1. Chester
2. Kaskaskia
3. Sparta

Union
1. Bald Knob Mountain
2. Cobden
3. Jonesboro

Washington
1. Nashville
2. Okawville

Williamson
1. Carterville
2. Marion

Alexander County

Cairo, the county seat of Alexander County, is where magnolia vies with the mimosa. The southernmost city in Illinois, it stands on the tip of a narrow peninsula where the Mississippi and Ohio rivers join on their journey to the Gulf of Mexico.

Cairo has many attractions for tourists to explore. The **Hewer,** Cairo's art treaure, is a heroic bronze nude by George Grey Barnard. It stands in Halliday Park between Ninth and Tenth streets. It was presented to the city in 1906 by Mrs. W.P. Halliday and her children in memory of Capt. W. P. Halliday. The statue reads: "A vision of men laboring on the shore of a flood hewing and dragging wood to save the people from death and destruction." Lorado Taft said the **Hewer** was one of the two finest nudes produced in America, the other being **Maidenhood.**

The **Cairo Public Library** contains several fine works of art. The building itself is an example of Queen Anne architecture. The leaded stained glass windows are original. In two niches at the entrance stand statues of Clio, the Greek muse, and Concordia, a Roman goddess of peace. A bronze fountain entitled **Fighting Boys** is the work of Janet Scudder, a famous American sculptor.

In the library reference room is a replica of the steamboat city of Cairo carved by a river pilot, Capt. Henry T. Ashton in 1876. On the first landing is a rare Tiffany grandfather's clock, one of only four of its type made by Tiffany.

Other artifacts are a chandelier originally hung in the Cairo Opera House, a desk belonging to President Andrew Jackson, cybis porcelains and a collection of fine paintings.

The library is open from 9 a.m.–5 p.m. Monday through Saturday. It is located at 1609 Washington Ave.

The **U.S. Customs House,** at Washington Avenue and Fifteenth Street, is a rare example of Palazzo or Commercial Italianate–style stone building. There are plans to reopen the building as a Civil War Museum and Cairo Tourism Office.

Magnolia Manor, 2700 Washington Ave., is a Victorian mansion and museum. It is open Thursday through Sunday 9 a.m.–5 p.m.; (618) 734-0201 or 734-3285.

The house is a four-storied red brick mansion of Italianate architecture. Large magnolia trees grace its lawn. There are fourteen rooms and a bed slept in by Gen. Ulysses S. Grant.

The **Magnolia Festival** is an annual event which celebrates the blooming of the magnolia trees in Cairo. Dances, concerts and other activities are held at the Magnolia Manor throughout the first week of May. Contact the Magnolia Manor for information.

Now a park, **Fort Defiance,** at Cairo Point, was a strategic site for settlement and fortification as early as 1673 when it was first sighted by explorers Jacques Marquette and Robert La Salle.

Where the Mississippi and Ohio rivers meet there is a single piece of mounted artillery. Starting in 1848, the cannon was used to greet arriving boats.

Fort Defiance State Park has facilities for picnicking and fishing on its 38 acres. The **Riverboat Memorial** is a triple-decked cement building resembling a square boat. The first deck is a sheltered picnic area with tables. The second and third decks provide outlooks; the second also supports the flagpole. For information contact Park Ranger, Box 77, Miller City, IL 62962; (618) 776-5281.

Mound City National Cemetery, four miles from the park, is a Civil War cemetery with 27 identified Confederate soldiers and 2,441 unknown ones.

The **Thebes Courthouse** in Thebes, west of SR 3 at Thebes Spur, is a brick and stone courthouse set precariously near the edge of a limestone bluff overlooking the town of Thebes and the Mississippi River. The courthouse was known as the "Courthouse on the Bluff." Here Dred Scott was imprisoned and Abraham Lincoln practiced law. It is an example of Greek Revival architecture and made of local materials. The courthouse is open in June and July, Monday through Friday from 9 a.m.–4 p.m.

Clinton County

Carlyle Lake, the largest inland lake in Illinois, lies primarily within the borders of Clinton County. Created in 1967 by damming the Kaskaskia River, its area covers some 24,580 acres with 83 miles of shoreline. The U.S. Army Corps of Engineers, which maintains the reservoir, estimates that more than 3½ million visitors enjoy the lake each year. Its primary attractions are fishing (for white bass, crappie, largemouth bass, channel catfish and bluegill), sailing, boating and hunting, in season. With two state parks on its shores—**Eldon Hazlet State Park** and **South Shore State Park**—camping is readily available.

More than 400 sites (336 with electric hookup) can be found in the state parks alone. Additional campsites are available at lake recreation areas and at commercial campgrounds. Eldon Hazlet State Park is off SR 127, six miles north of Carlyle. South Shore State Park is off U.S. 50, two miles east of Carlyle. The parks have the same phone number: (618) 594-3015.

A good place to begin a visit is the **Carlyle Visitor Center**, operated by the U.S. Army Corps of Engineers. The center displays a model of the lake and dam, showing how the reservoir was created. Exhibits of the area's natural history are especially informative. The center schedules worthwhile interpretive programs, such as nature walks, discussions of area Indian history and water safety seminars. Open Memorial Day through Labor Day 10 a.m.–4 p.m. Sunday through Thursday; 10 a.m.–6 p.m. Friday and Saturday. Open weekends in May and September; (618) 594-2484. The Carlyle Visitor Center is located at the Dam West recreation area, immediately west of the main dam one mile north of Carlyle off SR 127.

The **West Access Marina** supplies services to the lake's boaters—docking and fuel, motor and pontoon boat rental, Hobie Cats, sailboards and cabin sailboats for rent. A bait shop and restaurant serve Lake Carlyle sports enthusiasts. Harold and Mary Duffield, the proprietors, can be reached at (618) 594-2461. The marina is immediately west of the main dam, off SR 127 north of Carlyle.

Just south of the main dam, off SR 127, is a 1½-acre plot of natural prairie. In 1974, park rangers seeded the land with grasses and wildflowers indigenous to the Illinois prairie of 150 years ago. A one-mile trail leads through the prairie. Pick up a walking guide that explains the various plants at the Carlyle Visitor Center.

Carlyle even has its own entry in the *National Register of Historic Places*—the 1859 **General Dean suspension bridge,** the only suspension bridge in the state. Built to span the Kaskaskia River on the east side of town, the bridge was a link in the old St. Louis–Vincennes Trail. Stone towers 35 feet tall support a 280-foot span. The bridge was restored in 1977 for use as a pedestrian crossing. On the east side of the bridge is a recreation area with picnic tables and grills and a boat ramp. The bridge was named for William F. Dean, a Carlyle native and hero of the Korean War.

Franklin County

Franklin County shares its greatest natural resource, **Rend Lake**, with its neighbor, Jefferson County, to the north. Second largest in the state, the 18,900-acre lake has 162 miles of rugged shoreline, next to which is the 3,300-acre **Wayne Fitzgerrell State Park**. The park has 250 campsites, some with electric hookup, and offers a broad variety of recreational activities. For information, contact the Site Superintendent, Wayne Fitzgerrell State Park, SR 154 and I-57, Benton, IL 62812; (618) 439-3832. The park is open year-round.

The Rend Lake reservoir was created by damming the Big Muddy and Casey Fork rivers, giving it its unusual Y shape. The Army Corps of Engineers is responsible for the administration of the lake and its visitor center.

Crappie, bass and catfish are the most-caught species here. In season, hunting is available for all types of waterfowl, quail, pheasant, rabbit, deer and squirrel.

Families will enjoy the picnic areas scattered throughout the lake's recreation areas. The Sleepy Hollow Group Area is designed for disadvantaged and handicapped youth with advanced reservations. Swimming beaches are located at the South Sandusky and North Marcum Recreation Areas. The one marina on the west side of the lake has boat rentals available.

On the east side of the lake, the **Rend Lake Golf Course** is an 18-hole PGA facility with especially scenic terrain. Tennis courts, a restaurant and a championship trap shooting range are part of the club. Bird-watching is excellent here, as the lake is situated on the Mississippi Flyway, allowing the observer to view great migrations of geese and ducks and affording sightings of eagles, ospreys, loons, herons and other birds. In Wayne Fitzgerrell State Park, dog field trial grounds are host to regional and national championships. For information, contact the lake management office, (618) 724-2493.

In mid-May each year, the **Rend Lake Water Festival** features parades, a carnival, craft exhibits and entertainment. Call (618) 438-2121.

For all of us who love days off, Franklin County's seat, Benton, is where Memorial Day was first established. Here, **John A. Logan,** a Civil War major general, United States representative and senator and candidate for vice president in 1884, proposed the holiday in 1868, as commander of the Grand

Army of the Republic. A historical marker designates his home site at 204 S. Main St.

At the southern edge of the county, West Frankfort boasts a fine **Area Historical Museum** on 2000 E. St. Louis Street, with an old one-room schoolhouse, a mines and minerals display, and a program of events such as "Christmas on the Prairie" and "Brides Through the Decades." Each September, the museum puts on an "Apple Butter Stir," where the sweet stuff is made in huge copper kettles. It's usually all sold before it's finished cooking! The museum serves a tasty home-style lunch on Wednesday and Thursday from 11 a.m.–1 p.m., $2.25. Museum hours are 9 a.m.–4 p.m. Wednesday and Thursday and 1:30–4 p.m. on Sundays, closed January. Free admission; (618) 932-6159.

Jackson County

Carbondale, with a population of 26,000, is the largest city in the county and home to **Southern Illinois University** (founded in 1869). The college, with 24,000 students, is known for its sports teams, the Salukis, especially in basketball, which is played at SIU Arena, and football, at McAndrew Stadium. If you're in town during the season, be sure to catch a game with all its Southern Illinois enthusiasm. For tickets, contact Athletic Ticket Office, SIU, Carbondale, IL 62901; (618) 453-5319. The university's **Faner Museum and Art Galleries** have changing exhibits and works of special interest to Southern Illinois. Open daily Monday through Friday 9 a.m.–3 p.m., Sunday 1:30–4:30 p.m. Call (618) 453-2121.

With a name like Carbondale, one might guess that a primary industry hereabouts is coal mining. On the banks of the Big Muddy River, which flows to the west of Carbondale, was the first coal mining operation in Illinois. As early as 1810, the river bluffs supplied coal for local needs and to ship downriver to New Orleans. The beauty of the landscape, however, is largely undisturbed, with the Shawnee National Forest beginning just miles to the south and rivers and lakes all around.

Giant City State Park is located in the southeast corner of the county, 12 miles south of Carbondale off U.S. 51 and SR 13, with 3,700 acres of recreational area. The park takes its name from the huge sandstone formations here, such as the dramatic Devil's Stand-table, just west of the park's Interpretive Center.

The center has trained staff who will explain the various natural features of the park and present programs on its points of interest.

The Robinson cabin in the park is a reconstructed building that depicts life as it was in the area around 1880. An earlier structure, however, is the Stone Fort, a prehistoric stone wall at the top of an 80-foot sandstone cliff dating from 600–900 A.D. This is one of ten examples of such forts in southern Illinois, which may have been used for defense or ceremonial purposes.

Other evidence of prehistoric man in the region is found in rock shelters, whose roofs are presumably smoke-stained from camp fires. During the Civil War, these shelters were used by deserters from both sides.

A surprisingly modern construction in the park is the award-winning design of the park's 100,000-gallon spherical water tank. Eighty-two feet high, the tower has an observation platform with excellent views of the park. Some 50 feet up, the platform is reached by a spiral steel staircase.

Within the park is the 110-acre **Fern Rocks Nature Preserve,** where such rare plants as French's shooting star and large flowering mint may be found. Only hiking on the preserve's well-marked trail is allowed. Spring may be the best time to visit the park, for it is abloom with more than 170 different types of ferns and flowering plants. Birds abound in the park, as well, and make for excellent bird-watching.

Fishing is offered at **Little Grassy Lake,** adjacent to the park. There's picnicking and camping, too (161 sites, 117 with electric hookup). For information on Giant City State Park, contact the Site Superintendent, R.R. 1, Makanda, IL 62958; (618) 457-4836. You will receive a brochure that includes a short discussion of Little Grassy Lake. For a complete set of regulations governing the use of boats on this lake, however, write: Refuge Manager, Crab Orchard National Wildlife Refuge, Marion, IL 62958.

Noncampers will opt for the **Giant City Lodge and Cottages,** 34 rustic cabins in the state park, built of native stone. The dining room serves hearty meals around a handsome fireplace. There's a swimming pool here, too. Open March to mid-November; (618) 457-4921.

Jackson County's second major city is Murphysboro, the county seat. The apple is king here, with more than 31 commercial orchards in the vicinity. In fact, mid-September ushers in the annual **Apple Festival,** with pie-baking, apple-peeling and apple butter contests, a beauty pageant and a parade lead by Captain Applesauce. For dates and events, call the Chamber of Commerce at (618) 684-6421. Historically, Murphysboro claims the birthplace of Gen. John A. Logan, Civil War leader and United States Senator.

Lake Kincaid, northwest of Murphysboro, was created in 1972 by the state as a recreation area and water supply for the region. Its 2,750 acres, with 82 miles of timbered shoreline, serve those purposes admirably. Fishing, camping, boating, swimming and hunting in season are offered. Bass fishing is best during the months of April and May in this deep reservoir, bottoming out at 68 feet near the dam. Lake Kincaid is bounded by SR 149, SR 3 and SR 151 and is located approximately eight miles west of Murphysboro.

Two marinas service the boating public. One of them, **Kincaid Village Marina,** not only sells bait and tackle, but has boat rentals, a restaurant and campground; (618) 687-4914. To get there, travel west from Murphysboro on SR 149, approximately eight miles, to a blacktop road marked "To Kincaid Marina."

Lake Murphysboro State Park is situated about one mile west of Murphysboro off SR 149. The 904-acre park offers a number of recreational possibilities, from fishing to woodland hikes. An unusual feature of the park are patches of native wild orchids. Nine varieties grow here. Camping includes sites with electric hookups (77 sites total). Contact Site Superintendent, R.R. 4, Murphysboro, IL 62966; (618) 684-2867.

Cedar Lake, in the southern part of the county, is a 1,750-acre body of water only four miles south of Carbondale on SR 127.

Jefferson County

Jefferson County is filled with southern hospitality brought over the state line from Dixie. Mount Vernon, the county seat, was settled by southerners and remains peopled by the descendants of southern families.

Mount Vernon is also known as "The King City" because it "crowns southern Illinois."

A variety of activities await tourists, ranging from cultural activities, to historic sites, to sweet corn and watermelon festivals.

The **Mitchell Museum,** on the grounds of **Cedarhurst,** an 80-acre estate, has an 8,000-square-foot exhibit gallery, a smaller lecture gallery and storage for its extensive collection of nine-teenth- and twentieth-century American art collected by the late John R. and Eleanor Mitchell.

Exhibits specially selected by the Mitchell Museum rotate monthly and include traveling exhibits and annually scheduled shows featuring southern Illinois artists.

To reach the museum, from Broadway turn north at Twenty-Seventh Street, go east on Richview Road to the museum entrance. Museum hours are Tuesday through Saturday 10 a.m.–5 p.m., Sunday 1–5 p.m., closed Mondays and national holidays. For information, call (618) 242-1236.

Cedarhurst has several other attractions including hiking paths, a bird sanctuary, the Cedarhurst Arts Center and a nineteenth-century restored village. The Juniper Ridge Trail is a half-mile path around Mitchell Pond, and the Braille Trail has been developed for the sight-impaired. A shelter for bird observation is on the Juniper Ridge Trail.

The **Cedarhurst Arts Center** contains the county's first jail, a log structure built in 1820, and a log church dating from the 1870s. The Historical Society also has a small museum on the grounds and is open for special occasions.

Cedarhurst is open Tuesday through Sunday from 1–5 p.m., closed Mondays and national holidays. The Art Center is open Tuesday through Friday from 9 a.m.–4 p.m. Call (618) 244-6130.

The **Veterans Memorial Walkway** is a memorial to all Jefferson County soldiers killed in war. A special bronze plaque is mounted on granite for each soldier, and these granite stones border the County Courthouse at SR 37 and Main Street in downtown Mount Vernon. An eight-foot-tall black Carmelian granite monolith lists the wars in which Jefferson County citizens participated.

The **Appellate Courthouse** has plenty of history within its walls. Abraham Lincoln successfully argued a famous tax case in 1859, and Clara Barton used the building as a hospital in 1888. It is now the Fifth District Appellate Court and law library. Tours of the building are available when the court is not in session. It is located at Main and Fourteenth streets. Call (618) 242-3120 for information.

The newly remodeled **Brehm Memorial Library** houses

historical documents regarding local history and genealogy. It is located at 101 South Seventh St., and its summer hours are Monday through Friday 9 a.m.–8 p.m., Saturday 11 a.m.–5 p.m., Sunday 1–5 p.m.; (618) 242-6322.

The **Sweet Corn and Watermelon Festival** is held the third week in August. A week of activities includes free sweet corn and watermelon served in the town square. Contact the Mount Vernon Convention and Visitors Bureau, P.O. Box 2580, Mount Vernon, IL 62864; (618) 242-3151.

As well as providing 9 to 11 million gallons of water daily for the area, **Rend Lake** provides a recreational retreat. The lake is surrounded by rolling hill prairie country and has excellent crappie fishing. Waterfowl are hunted here as well as deer, rabbit, dove, quail, pheasant and squirrel.

Picnic grounds for both small and large groups are adjacent to the lake, and Sleepy Hollow Group Area is designed for handicapped and disadvantaged youth groups. Advance reservations are necessary for that area.

Beaches are located at the South Sandusky Recreation Area and North Marcum Recreation Area. There are many boat launching facilities for sail and motorboats, and a marina is located on the west side of the lake.

An 18-hole golf course, tennis courts, pro shop, trap shooting, restaurant and meeting rooms are also available to tourists.

Observation of geese and duck, eagles, osprey, loon, swans, heron and songbirds on the Mississippi Flyway is a special treat for bird-watchers.

For information contact the U.S. Army Corps of Engineers, Rend Lake Management Office, R.R. 3, Benton, IL 62812, (618) 724-2493 or Rend Lake Conservancy District, P.O. Box 497, Benton, IL 62812, (618) 439-4321.

Johnson County

Johnson County is a paradise for those interested in Indian history and nature.

Buffalo Rock, three miles northeast of Simpson off SR 147 toward Reynoldsburg, has the outline of a buffalo etched into the side of a sandstone cliff. Indians are said to be the artists responsible for this drawing. The trail leading to the site is filled with lovely beech and sugar maple trees, and dozens of colorful wildflowers carpet the forest floor in spring.

The **Milestone Bluff,** north off SR 147 at Robbs, is an ancient Indian dwelling and burial site. The bluff has a prehistoric stone wall and Indian grave sites. The Mississippi Indians are believed to have inhabited the area from 1000 to 1500 A.D. The hiking trail to the bluff begins at the parking lot.

The **Rainbow Arch,** less than one mile west of Cypress off SR 37, is a bridge of sandstone rock surrounded by beautiful white and red oak trees and wild black cherries. One of the largest natural bridges in southern Illinois, it is 66 feet long, 3½ feet wide and 7 feet high at its peak.

The **River-to-River Trail,** east off U.S. 45, 3½ miles north of I-24 at Vienna, is a dirt trail stretching nearly halfway around the entire southern tip of Illinois. Three connecting trails make it more than 23 miles long. Plans are being made to extend the trail over the entire southern end of Illinois.

The **Penn Central Tunnel,** one mile west off U.S. 45 and six miles north of I-24 at Vienna, is one of the oldest stretches of track still in operation. Original construction of the tunnel began in 1871–72 when a tunnel was blasted 800 feet through sandstone and shale. Speed on the track is restricted to 5 mph in the tunnel, 8 mph on the open track. Despite track conditions, one train still makes a daily run.

The **Little Black Slough Natural Area,** half a mile east of SR 37 and SR 146, is unusual for its terrain. The area is a mixture of primeval tupelo and cypress swamps, rich floodplain forest and upland woods with small patches of limestone prairie glades.

Some of the oldest living trees east of the Mississippi River are here, and a boardwalk allows access to the heart of the swamp. Nine miles of hiking trails wind through Little Black Slough, and the towering tupelo and cypress trees rising from the swamp make it a unique site in Illinois.

For information about both Little Black Slough Natural Area and the following attraction, contact the Site Superintendent, Ferne Clyffe State Park, P.O. Box 120, Goreville, IL 62939; (618) 995-2411.

Ferne Clyffe State Park, one mile south of Goreville, has more than 1,000 acres of the largest bluffs and caves in the area. A 16-acre fishing lake is within the park.

The park has a central valley from which radiate gorges and canyons. Shady dells, natural cathedrals, domes, brooks, cascades and rills have formed here. Several so-called caves are not really caves but great protruding ledges of rock that make an arched roof.

Hawks Cave is a sheer cliff of stone so hewn by wind and water that an excavation has been made at its base at least 150 feet long and as many feet high. The cave has a natural pulpit and excellent acoustics.

Park facilities include picnicking, fishing, camping and horseback riding trails.

Vienna can't live up to the expectations of its name, but it does have some attractions worth seeing. The **Vienna Times Building** is beautifully preserved. It was built around 1890 as a bank, and in 1915 the Vienna Times Newspaper took it over. It is at the Vienna public square four blocks west of the junction of SR 146W and U.S. 45 at the corner of East Main and Fourth streets. It is open to the public during business hours.

The **Paul Powell Home,** also four blocks west of this junction at 404 Vine St., is the home of former Illinois Secretary of State and Illinois Representative Paul Powell. The house is completely furnished and is open year-round on Saturday and Sunday 2–4 p.m. A historical museum is located in the basement of the house.

Marion County

The Midwest has few stories about earthquakes, but Salem, surprisingly, was founded as a result of the New Madrid, Missouri, earthquake of 1811. The quake was so powerful that it caused the Mississippi River to flow backwards and sent Capt. Samuel Young in search of a less shaky home. Young came to Marion County and found an abundance of game and tranquility. He made his camp on what is now the courthouse square in Salem.

Salem became a stagecoach stop on the Vincennes Trail, and the arrival of the railroads in 1850 and 1860 produced Salem's first boom. In the early 1900s, oil brought another boom to the town, and in 1939, Salem was the nation's second largest oilfield.

Salem also has some prominent history in its veins. **William Jennings Bryan,** called the Silver-Tongued Orator and the Great Commoner, was born here. He was the United States Secretary of State, 1913–15, and three-time presidential candidate. His **birthplace** is now a museum located near the public library, which also bears his name.

"Ingram's Log Cabin," Kinmundy

Salem's American Legion Post was a pioneer in producing the GI Bill of Rights. It took seven months and eight days from the time the Salem Legionnaires collaborated on the plan until it was approved by Congress in 1944.

Salem is full of historic architecture and the Chamber of Commerce, 210 W. Main St., Salem, IL 62881, (618) 548-3010, has published a walking tour that highlights the sites. The tour begins at North Broadway and Boone streets and takes you through a former **stagecoach station, Max Corsset's Cafe** (home of Miracle Whip Salad Dressing, which was sold to Kraft Foods in 1931 for $300), past the **Marion County Courthouse,** a statue of William Jennings Bryan by Gutzon Borglum, (famed sculptor of Mount Rushmore), and the **Silas Bryan Farm,** former home of Williams Jennings Bryan. A separate tour of the home is available.

The tour continues on through several homes of the 1800s

and 1900s and ends at Bryan's birthplace. The map is available at the Chamber of Commerce.

Other historic sites near Salem are the **One-Room School-house,** Salem Community High School campus, SR 37 North. This one-room schoolhouse has been refurbished to illustrate educational facilities during the nineteenth and early twentieth centuries. It is open 2–4 p.m. on Saturday from April 1 through October, other times by appointment; (618) 548-2799.

The **Halfway Tavern,** ten miles east of Salem on U.S. 50 East, was built in 1818 and originally served as a stagecoach stop until 1861. It was on the trail across Illinois used by Capt. George Rogers Clark in 1799 and Abraham Lincoln used it as a stopover.

Oil was first discovered near Salem in 1909, but the oil boom came in 1938. The Salem Oilfield ranked 17th in the nation in volume of oil production. It currently produces more than 3,000,000 barrels a year. Pumps can be seen at the field six miles southwest of Salem.

Ingram's Log Cabin Village in Kinmundy, northeast of Salem, has 13 authentic log buildings dating from 1818 to 1860. Ten of the buildings are authentically furnished and open to the public. The village is on 65 acres of land with a seven-acre lake.

The Inn is a large, two-story building, once a stagecoach stop. There are several homes, Millican's grocery store and post office, an apothecary, cobbler's shop and church.

Admission is $1.25 for adults, 75 cents for high school students, 50 cents for junior high school students, and 25 cents for kindergartners through fifth grade. Hours are 9:30 a.m.–5:30 p.m. daily, April 15th through November 15th. Contact Ingram's Log Cabin Village, Kinmundy, IL 62854; (618) 547-7123.

The **Stephen A. Forbes State Fish and Wildlife Area,** 14 miles northeast of Salem, has outdoor recreation including fishing, hunting, boating, picnicking, waterskiing, swimming, camping, hiking and horseback riding. A Fisheries Research Center conducts aquatic biology and fisheries experiments. The center is open to visitors Monday through Friday 7 a.m.–4 p.m. Tours can be arranged by calling (618) 245-6848.

For information about the park, contact the Site Superintendent, Stephen A. Forbes State Fish and Wildlife Area, R.R. 1, Kinmundy, IL 62865; (618) 547-3381.

Perry County

Du Quoin got its start as a stopping point on the old Shawneetown-to-Kaskaskia Road, where there was a crossing at the Little Muddy River. The town took its name from Kaskaskia Indian Chief Jean Baptiste Ducoigne, who came to the aid of George Rogers Clark after the fall of Kaskaskia and later served in the Revolutionary Army under Lafayette in Virginia. His tribe camped near the spot of the first white settlement, which took his name. When the railroad came to town in 1853, the town site moved a short distance to its present location.

Today, the area is an important center for agriculture and mining and the largest coal-producing county in Illinois. Numerous strip mines are found throughout the region. Du Quoin's major annual event is the **Du Quoin State Fair,** which begins ten days prior to Labor Day and runs through the holiday. Over 200,000 visitors are attracted to the more-than-60-years-old event. Name entertainment, championship auto racing, and world-class harness racing headline the fair. The fairground's dirt track is called the "Magic Mile" for the number of speed records that have been set here. Tractor pulls and livestock shows round out the schedule. Throughout the year, other events are staged at the fairgrounds, including camping rallies and a rodeo. Contact the Du Quoin State Fairgrounds at P.O. Box 191, Du Quoin, IL 62832; (618) 542-9373.

After the fair, or any time, dinner at **Siefert's** is always a treat. Located at U.S. 51 and SR 14, the restaurant, run by proprietor Tom Siefert, serves some of the best fish in the area—blackened redfish and sole strips are recommended. Closed Sunday; (618) 542-8911. Prices range from $8–$12.

Randolph County

Randolph is one of the most historically and geographically unique counties in all of Illinois. A tiny appendage protruding into the main body of Missouri, Kaskaskia Island is the only part of the state lying *west* of the Mississippi River.

Kaskaskia is the second oldest settlement (after Cahokia) in the state, founded as a Jesuit mission in 1703. Thus, the area's French heritage is rich. Fort Kaskaskia was erected in the village and served as an outpost in the French and Indian War (1754–63).

Covered Bridge   Mary's River Near Chester

After the Treaty of Paris in 1763, the region came under British control. In 1778, George Rogers Clark captured the settlement for America, and it became a county of Virginia. In 1787 it became part of the new Northwest Territory, in 1800 part of the Indiana Territory, in 1809 the capital of the Illinois Territory, and the first state capital in 1818 (to 1820 when it moved to Vandalia).

Kaskaskia declined in importance, and Mississippi floods around 1885 eventually destroyed the old settlement, cutting a new channel for the Mississippi through the heart of the town, creating Kaskaskia Island on the western side.

What remained on the eastern side of the river is now **Fort Kaskaskia State Park;** (618) 859-3741. The park is an especially scenic area with places for picnicking among the trees. Situated on a hill, it overlooks the Mississippi River and Kaskaskia Island.

Just below the park, at the foot of the hill, between Chester and Ellis Grove, off SR 3, is the **Pierre Menard Home,** now a state memorial. Built in 1802 in French Colonial style, with a wide gallery porch and a low, hipped roof, this was the residence of the first lieutenant governor of Illinois, one of the most important men in the history of the territory. In 1824 he entertained the visiting hero Lafayette. The house has been restored and furnished with pieces of the period. Open daily except Thanksgiving, Christmas and New Year's Day; (618) 859-3031. The museum is free to the public, with hours from 9 a.m.–5 p.m.

On Kaskaskia Island is the **Liberty Bell of the West,** a gift from Louis XV of France. Today, it's a state memorial. To reach the island, cross the Chester toll bridge at SR 51 and travel 12 miles to St. Mary's, Missouri, then follow the directional signs to the island.

Chester, the county seat, is the site of **Greenwood Cemetery,** where Shadrach Bond, the first governor of the state (1818–22) is buried. A white granite monument erected by the state in 1883 marks the gravesite.

Chester, too, is home to Popeye. His creator, Elzie Crisler Segar, was born here in 1894. In 1977, a statue of the lovable sailorman was erected in **Segar Memorial Park. A Popeye Picnic and Parade** are usually held the first weekend in September.

North of Chester on SR 3, the Colvis and Gross families have large **orchards** with peaches, apples and strawberries for sale. At the Colvis Orchard, you can view apple cider being pressed.

Seven miles east of Chester on SR 150 between Chester and Bremen, is one of the state's few **covered bridges,** over Mary's River. The 98-foot single-span bridge of hand-hewn native oak was erected in 1854.

North of Chester and Fort Kaskaskia are Prairie du Rocher (field of the rock) and **Fort de Chartres.** No missionary is responsible for the settlement here. Instead, credit goes to an early entrepreneur who set the stage for a long line of American land speculators to follow. John Law was a Scotch businessman who obtained a charter from the French government to colonize the region. His Company of the West brought in immigrants from France, Italy, Switzerland and Germany. Law promised speculators great profits, but his "Mississippi Bubble" burst in 1720, leaving the settlers stranded.

Most stayed, under the protection of Pierre Duque, Sieur de Boisbriant, commandant of the Illinois country. By 1720, he completed the construction of Fort de Chartres, named for the Duc de Chartres, son of the French regent. The fort was rebuilt three times, and in its final form was considered one of the strongest in North America.

Today, parts of the old fort have been reconstructed and are part of a state park. Each year in June, the **Fort de Chartres Rendezvous** recreates life in the French era with volunteers in militia uniforms, a fife and drum corps, much firing of cannon and French Colonial cooking. Fort de Chartres is open year-round, 9 a.m.–5 p.m. Admission is free; (618) 284-7230.

In the northeast corner of the county, at Sparta, is the **Charter Oak School,** one of only a few octagonal schoolhouses remaining in the United States. Built in 1873, it served its public purpose until 1953.

From Sparta, head south on SR 4 to the Schuline Crossroads, about four miles, turn right, then seven miles down a country road. A distinctly modern counterpoint is the **Sparta Archway Parachute Club,** which offers skydiving from the airport here.

From Chester, U.S. Bicycle Route 76 leads east to Shiloh Hill and the county line, along scenic back roads. Also out in the country is **Kloth's Antiques,** one of the county's better collectible shops, located at the junction of SR 4 and SR 150, two miles west of Steeleville.

Union County

Between mid-December of 1838 and early March 1839, 10,000 Cherokee Indians were forced to travel 800 miles from their home in the Great Smoky Mountains to a reservation in present day Oklahoma. The exiled Cherokees stopped in southern Illinois because of floating ice on the Mississippi River and made camp. The camps provided little shelter against the unusually severe winter that year and many died, giving the area the name "Trail of Tears."

Trail of Tears State Forest, formerly Union State Forest, is northwest of Jonesboro near the Mississippi River. It lies within the beautiful Shawnee Hill country and is a preserve to protect native tree species of Illinois. Approximately 60 acres are devoted to the Union State Tree Nursery, and nearly all species of trees in southern Illinois are found here.

The park has picnicking facilities, approximately 44 trails totaling more than 36 miles, hunting and tent camping. You can reach the park by taking SR 3 to Wolf Lake, then drive east for five miles. For information call (618) 833-4910.

The **Union County Conservation Area** is in the Lower Mississippi River Bottomlands Division of Illinois. It is a haven for wildlife and most prominent throughout five months of the year is the flock of Canada geese and other waterfowl that winter in the area. No hunting is allowed and there are no overnight facilities. This conservation area is southwest of Jonesboro off SR 3 near Reynoldsville. For information contact the Union County Conservation Area, R.R. 2, Jonesboro, IL 62952; (618) 833-5175.

The **Cobden Museum** in Cobden, affectionately known as the Appleknocker Town, was opened by three amateur archeologists who spent more than 30 years searching for Indian artifacts in the southern Illinois area. They stored the finds in a basement and soon outgrew the space. Apparently, the wives of the amateurs did not like having Indian skeletons and grave goods in their basements and told their husbands to move the stuff. The men decided to open a museum.

Museum hours are 9–11 a.m. and 1–4:30 p.m. Monday through Saturday, and 1–4:30 p.m. on Sunday; (618) 893-2067. It is advisable for visitors to call to make sure the museum is open. It usually closes for the winter in late November and reopens in March. Admission is free but donations are welcomed.

Bald Knob Mountain, four miles West of Alto Pass, has local talent performing Passion Plays. Performances are July through September every Friday and Saturday at 8:30 p.m. Call (618) 893-2344 for information.

Washington County

Perhaps one of the most unusual hotels in the state is the **Original Mineral Springs Hotel and Bath House** in Okawville, just off I-64 in the northwest part of the county. Built in 1892, the 56-room hostelry is listed in the *National Register of Historic Places.* For more than 90 years, guests have been coming for the relaxing mineral water baths. Book a Swedish massage and a therapeutic soak when you visit. Open year-round: rates for a double, $25–$45, (618) 243-5458.

The **Okawville Heritage House and Museum,** too, is listed in the *National Register,* and gives the visitor an idea of life in the last century. Open noon–4 p.m. Saturday and Sunday.

Nashville is the county seat, named after the hometown of the first settlers from Tennessee. In the northeast part of the city, on 37 acres of rolling wooded land, **Nashville Memorial Park** is a center for outdoor recreational activity. A new swimming complex with separate areas for diving, toddlers and intermediate swimmers was completed in 1981. The pool can accommodate 371 on a busy summer day. The park's other facilities include four baseball diamonds, tennis courts, a playground, picnic areas and even a challenging par-36 nine-hole municipal golf course.

In town, the **First Presbyterian Church**, 300 W. St. Louis St., is one of the oldest churches in Illinois. Organized in 1832, the present church building dates from 1884.

The **Washington County Historical Society Museum**, 300 S. Kaskaskia St., houses artifacts and exhibits relative to the history of the area. The museum is open Sunday 1:30–3:30 p.m. or by appointment. The historical society also maintains the historic **McKelvey one-room schoolhouse** just west of town (open by appointment only).

Collectors will want to visit **Antiques and Elderly Things,** 100 E. St. Louis, Nashville's favorite spot for treasure hunters.

Or, plan a visit on the third week in September when Nashville holds its yearly **Fall Festival Days** on the courthouse square, complete with music, food and crafts.

Four miles south of Nashville, off SR 127, is the **Washington County Conservation Area,** a 1,377-acre preserve set in rolling wooded hills. A central part of the area is a 248-acre lake with 13 miles of shoreline. Bass, bluegill, crappie and catfish are the most frequently caught species. The lake, which has a 10 horsepower limit, has launch ramps and a marina, which rents boats and motors and sells tackle, bait and snacks. A 14-mile trail winds through the woods of the conservation area. Campers, too, can enjoy the habitat, with campsites for tent camping and those with full facilities (including electric hookups and showers). Nine hundred acres are posted for seasonal shotgun and bow and arrow hunting. The park is accessible year-round.

Williamson County

Crab Orchard National Wildlife Refuge was started in the

1930s when the government had rows of pine trees planted to provide work for the WPA (Works Project Administration) and the Civilian Conservation Corps. In 1947, the refuge was officially established by the Department of the Interior and now covers 43,000 acres. The area includes three lakes, 12 natural areas and a 4,000-acre wilderness area.

Forest, prairie and wetland plants and animals live harmoniously in Crab Orchard. Wildlife management is centered around providing winter feeding and resting areas for Canada geese, and the refuge's goose flock may build up to 120,000 birds by December. Many species of ducks and bald eagles can be seen in the trees overlooking the goose flock.

Spring brings most of the migratory waterfowl and eagles. Whitetail deer (common year-round), coyotes, beaver, muskrat, opossum and raccoon also inhabit the area. A bird list is available at the refuge headquarters.

Wildlife-oriented recreation is encouraged, and the opportunities for wildlife observation are excellent. For hikers there is the self-guided **Chamnesstown School Trail.** The trail explores a reconstructed schoolhouse and ventures out along old fire trails in open areas of the refuge. Observation towers are wonderful lookouts for watching geese, and there are picnicking areas by **Crab Orchard Lake.**

Hunting and fishing are allowed, and there is a concession-operated campground and marina as well as swimming.

The refuge is located between Carbondale and Marion, accessible from I-57. Visitors are permitted only in designated areas. The refuge headquarters is open 7 a.m.–4 p.m. Monday through Friday. For information contact the Project Manager, Crab Orchard National Wildlife Refuge, P.O. Box J, Carterville, IL 62918; (618) 997-3344.

Little Grassy Fish Hatchery, downstream of Little Grassy Lake, is a 115-acre hatchery with a visitors observation area where you can view rearing, spawning and egg incubation tanks.

The warm water hatchery combines two methods of fish rearing, intensive and extensive culture. Intensive culture uses a high water exchange through a rearing unit for environmental control and allows rearing of large numbers of fish per unit. Extensive culture uses earthen ponds, an extension of nature, but with some control as to the number of fish per pond and the food organisms available.

The original hatchery was built in 1959, and expansion and

modernization began in July, 1979, as a result of a state study of projected demands for fish stocking.

Largemouth bass, bluegill, redear sunfish and channel catfish are reared here as well as some smallmouth bass, walleye, muskellunge, northern pike and striped bass.

The hatchery is southeast of Carbondale and accessible via Little Grassy Road. It is within the boundaries of Crab Orchard Wildlife Refuge. Visitor tours are on a self-guided basis though employee-guided tours can be scheduled for large groups. Hours are 8:30 a.m.–3:30 p.m. daily; (618) 529-4100.

Nearby Marion has a quaint little shopping and dining house called **Collector's Choice,** 500 S. Court St.; (618) 997-4883. Eleven shops each represent some of the most talented area artists, crafts people, antique dealers and collectors. A country store takes you back to the era of ice cream parlors, and a tearoom features gourmet entrees. Hours for the stores are Monday through Friday 10 a.m.–5 p.m., Saturday 10 a.m.–3 p.m., and closed Sunday. Tearoom hours are 11 a.m.–2 p.m. daily, closed on Sunday.

Index

Index

Index